COMMON CORE
English Language Arts

in a PLC at Work™

GRADES K-2

DOUGLAS FISHER
NANCY FREY

Foreword by Rebecca DuFour

A Joint Publication With

INTERNATIONAL
Reading
Association

555 North Morton Street
Bloomington, IN 47404
800.733.6786 (toll free) / 812.336.7700
FAX: 812.336.7790

email: info@solution-tree.com
solution-tree.com

Visit **go.solution-tree.com/commoncore** to download the reproducibles in this book.

Printed in the United States of America

16 15 14 13   4 5

IRA Stock No. 9245

Library of Congress Cataloging-in-Publication Data

Fisher, Douglas, 1965-
  Common core English language arts in a PLC at work, grades K-2 / Douglas Fisher, Nancy Frey.
      pages cm
  "A joint publication with IRA."
  "IRA Stock No. 9245."
  Includes bibliographical references and index.
  ISBN 978-1-936764-16-7 (perfect bound) 1. Language arts (Elementary)--Standards--United States. 2. Language arts (Elementary)--Curricula--United States. 3. Professional learning communities. I. Title.
  LB1576.F4419 2013
  372.6'044--dc23
                              2012038787

Solution Tree
Jeffrey C. Jones, CEO
Edmund M. Ackerman, President

Solution Tree Press
President: Douglas M. Rife
Publisher: Robert D. Clouse
Editorial Director: Lesley Bolton
Managing Production Editor: Caroline Wise
Senior Production Editor: Joan Irwin
Copy Editor: Sarah Payne-Mills
Proofreader: Elisabeth Abrams
Cover and Text Designer: Jenn Taylor

TABLE OF CONTENTS

ABOUT THE AUTHORS

 **Douglas Fisher**, PhD, is a professor of educational leadership at San Diego State University and a teacher leader at Health Sciences High and Middle College. He teaches courses in instructional improvement. As a classroom teacher, Fisher focuses on English language arts instruction. He also serves as the literacy instructional advisor to the Chula Vista Elementary School District.

Fisher received an International Reading Association Celebrate Literacy Award for his work on literacy leadership and was elected to the board of directors in 2012. For his work as codirector of the City Heights Professional Development Schools, Fisher received the Christa McAuliffe award. He was corecipient of the Farmer Award for excellence in writing from the National Council of Teachers of English for the article, "Using Graphic Novels, Anime, and the Internet in an Urban High School," published in the *English Journal*.

Fisher has written numerous articles on reading and literacy, differentiated instruction, and curriculum design. His books include *In a Reading State of Mind*, *Checking for Understanding*, *Better Learning Through Structured Teaching*, and *Text Complexity*.

He earned a bachelor's degree in communication, a master's degree in public health education, and a doctoral degree in multicultural education. Fisher completed post-doctoral study at the National Association of State Boards of Education focused on standards-based reforms.

Nancy Frey, PhD, is a professor of literacy in the School of Teacher Education at San Diego State University. Through the university's teacher-credentialing and reading specialist programs, she teaches courses on elementary and secondary reading instruction and literacy in content areas, classroom management, and supporting students with diverse learning needs. Frey also teaches at Health Sciences High and Middle College in San Diego. She was a board member of the California Reading Association and a credentialed special educator, reading specialist, and administrator in California.

Before joining the university faculty, Frey was a public school teacher in Florida. She worked at the state level for the Florida Inclusion Network helping districts design systems for supporting students with disabilities in general education classrooms.

She is the recipient of the 2008 Early Career Achievement Award from the National Reading Conference and the Christa McAuliffe Award for excellence in teacher education from the American Association of State Colleges and Universities. She was corecipient of the Farmer Award for excellence in writing from the National Council of Teachers of English for the article "Using Graphic Novels, Anime, and the Internet in an Urban High School."

Frey is author of *The Formative Assessment Action Plan*, *Productive Group Work*, *Teaching Students to Read Like Detectives*, and *Content-Area Conversations*. She has written articles for *The Reading Teacher*, *Journal of Adolescent and Adult Literacy*, *English Journal*, *Voices From the Middle*, *Middle School Journal*, *Remedial and Special Education*, and *Educational Leadership*.

To book Douglas Fisher or Nancy Frey for professional development, contact pd@solution-tree.com.

FOREWORD

The publication of *Common Core English Language Arts in a PLC at Work™, Grades K–2* could not be more timely as educators across the United States are gearing up to make the new standards the foundation of their English language arts (ELA) curriculum, instruction, assessment, intervention, enrichment, and professional development processes. The authors, Douglas Fisher and Nancy Frey, are not only two of the United States' most highly regarded experts in ELA but are also educators who have a deep understanding of the steps needed to bring the Common Core standards to life in our classrooms. Fisher and Frey recognize that if students are going to learn these rigorous skills, concepts, and ways of thinking that are essential to their current and future success, then the educators serving those students must no longer work in traditional isolated classrooms but rather must work as members of collaborative teams in schools and districts that function as professional learning communities (PLCs). As the authors state on page 4:

> In fact, chances are good that you are interested in this book because it promises to link an important change—implementing the Common Core State Standards in English language arts—with a process you already know to be powerful: professional learning communities.

Picture an elementary teacher working in a traditional school. He or she will likely be provided a copy of the Common Core State Standards document, may receive a few hours of training from someone in the district, and then essentially will be left to work in isolation for the rest of the year to interpret, teach, and assess each standard to the best of his or her ability. The degree to which the students assigned into that traditional classroom learn each standard will almost exclusively depend on that teacher's understanding of each standard, how much time and energy he or she is able and willing to devote to the new standards, and finally, his or her ability to teach the standards effectively.

Now imagine a team of teachers working in a school that embraces the PLC at Work process. Team members will be provided a copy of the Common Core ELA document and will work together collaboratively to develop a common understanding of what the standards entail. They will be provided time and support to study and discuss each standard in order to clarify, sequence, pace, and assess the standards in a common way across each grade level. Each team will be provided time to collaborate vertically with teams in the grade levels above and below its own to build a strong scope and sequence and a common language for ELA as students progress from one grade to the next. Leadership at the school and district levels will not only provide each team with the necessary time, support, and ongoing training to engage in this critical collaborative work but also put structures in place and empower staffs to build schoolwide systems of intervention, extension, and enrichment for students—providing time and support for each student to take his or her own learning to the next level.

I am confident this book, written by two respected colleagues, will provide you—my heroes working in schools and districts each day—with ideas, strategies, tools, and resources to help you bring the Common Core English language arts standards to life in your classrooms. The students entrusted to you deserve nothing less.

—Rebecca DuFour

INTRODUCTION

The investment of time and expertise by schools and districts to make the transformation into an effective Professional Learning Community (PLC) at Work™ is about to pay off once again. The adoption of the Common Core State Standards for English language arts (CCSS ELA) represents a significant change in how the education profession looks at curriculum, instruction, and assessment. In addition, the implications for implementation of the CCSS ELA will have ramifications for years to come. As new research on best practices related to the Common Core State Standards is conducted and disseminated, educators will need to interpret these results and determine how best to put them into practice. The PLC process offers an ideal foundational system for doing so. This process provides the necessary conditions and support to accomplish the work of ensuring continuous improvement. Ongoing professional development is embedded into the process, because teachers work as members of high-performing collaborative teams. Becoming a PLC is a process of reculturing a school; the concept is not just another meeting (DuFour, DuFour, & Eaker, 2008; Frey, Fisher, & Everlove, 2009). Effective districtwide or schoolwide PLCs have the following six characteristics (DuFour et al., 2008; DuFour, DuFour, Eaker, & Many, 2010).

1. **Shared mission, vision, values, and goals all focused on student learning:** The *mission* defines why the organization exists; the *vision* defines what the organization can become in the future; the *values* consist of demonstrated attitudes and behaviors that further the vision; and the *goals* are markers used to determine results and assess progress. A thriving PLC immerses itself in the behaviors necessary to the development of these concepts.

2. **A collaborative culture with a focus on learning:** *Collaboration*, an essential ingredient in the PLC process, enables people to work interdependently to improve teaching and learning.

3. **Collective inquiry into best practice and current reality:** *Collective inquiry* is the process through which PLC educators strive to build shared knowledge about research and what works in their classrooms.

4. **Action orientation:** An *action orientation* is characteristic of successful PLCs that learn by doing and recognize the significance and necessity of actions that engage their members in planning learning tasks, implementing them, and evaluating results.

5. **A commitment to continuous improvement:** *Continuous improvement* is a cyclical process that PLCs use to plan, implement, and check to determine the effectiveness of their efforts to improve teaching and learning.

6. **Results orientation:** *Results* are what count for PLCs; they are the measurable outcomes that reveal the success of the collaborative efforts to improve teaching and learning. Results outweigh intentions.

Visit **www.allthingsplc.info** for a glossary of PLC terms.

These six characteristics must be woven into the fabric of the school; they have to become part of the air that teachers, parents, students, and administrators breathe. In creating this culture, PLCs must reach agreement on fundamental issues, including (DuFour et al., 2008):

- What content students should learn

- What common and coherent assessments to develop and use to determine if students have learned the agreed-on curriculum

- How to respond when students do or don't learn the agreed-on curriculum

To accomplish these three tasks, teachers need adequate time to collaborate with their colleagues. We are not suggesting that scheduling time for teachers to collaborate is easy, but without dedicated time, teams will not develop the collaborative structures needed to support student learning, especially if teachers are going to address the Common Core State Standards in grades K–2. As part of their collaborative team time, teachers in PLCs engage in inquiry into student learning. The following four critical questions of a PLC highlight and provide a foundation for the work of collaborative planning teams (DuFour et al., 2008).

1. What do we want our students to learn?

2. How will we know when they have learned it?

3. How will we respond when some students don't learn?

4. How will we extend and enrich the learning for students who are already proficient?

Professional Development and Professional Learning Communities

Linda Darling-Hammond (2010) summarizes the research on effective professional development as follows:

> Effective professional development is sustained, ongoing, content-focused, and embedded in professional learning communities where teachers work overtime on problems of practice with other teachers in their subject area or school. Furthermore, it focuses on concrete tasks of teaching, assessment, observation, and reflection, looking at how students learn specific content in particular contexts. . . . It is often useful for teachers to be put in the position of studying the very material that they intend to teach to their own students. (pp. 226–227)

In other words, effective professional development is often the opposite of what most teachers receive—it is sustained and embedded within the work of professional learning communities and focused on the actual tasks of teaching using the material teachers use with students. Professional development practices have moved beyond stand-alone workshops to ones that are tied to a school's chosen area of focus. Through the work of researchers like Bruce Joyce and Beverly Showers (1983) and others, educators began to understand that professional development could be linked to the change process. In particular, the value of an agreed-on focus, the need for continued support after the session, and a plan for measuring success have become expected elements of any school's professional development plan. To succeed as a high-performance school, professional development should be part of a teacher's overall involvement in a learning community.

The link between professional development and school change has been further strengthened through PLCs (Eaker, DuFour, & DuFour, 2002). PLCs recognize that teacher collaboration lies at the heart of learning and change. Collaborative planning teams within PLCs are able to bridge theory to practice as they convene regularly to examine student performance data, discuss student progress, develop and implement curricula, and coach one another through meaningful collaborative work between meetings.

The evidence of PLC effectiveness is mounting. A study of elementary teachers in PLCs identifies a strong statistical correlation between their participation in professional learning communities, their classroom cultures, and their use of formative assessments to advance learning (Birenbaum, Kimron, & Shilton, 2011). Robert Bullough and Steven Baugh (2008) find that the conditions created to foster a schoolwide PLC in turn deepened a school-university partnership. In an analysis of nearly four hundred schools as PLCs, Louise Stoll, Ray Bolam, Agnes McMahon, Mike Wallace, and Sally Thomas (2006) note a positive relationship between student achievement, adoption of innovative practices, and healthy learning communities. In fact, Robert Marzano notes that school and district-level PLCs are "probably the most influential movement with regards to actually changing practices in schools" (DuFour & Marzano, 2011, p. x).

Purpose of This Book

We hope we have made the case, however, briefly, that a PLC at the school or district level is vital to school change. Furthermore, collaborative planning teams functioning within the school's PLC provide embedded professional development that sustains change.

In fact, chances are good that you are interested in this book because it promises to link an important change—implementing the Common Core State Standards in English language arts—with a process you already know to be powerful: professional learning communities. The remainder of this book provides collaborative teacher teams with information about the *what* and the *how* of teaching students to master these standards, including how to develop effective formative assessment and respond when students fail to make progress. We expand the Common Core standards so that you and your team can examine them in detail. You will find that each chapter begins with questions for your team to consider, and we invite you to return to these after you examine the standards to discuss implications for instruction, curriculum, assessment, and intervention.

Organization of This Book

This book has been crafted with your collaborative team in mind. Use it as a workbook—mark it up, dog-ear the pages, highlight passages that resonate, underline the ones that raise a question. In the same way that the Common Core ELA standards focus our collective attention on the practices of close reading and argumentation, we hope to contribute to a similar process for your team. The conversation begins in chapter 1 with an overview of the CCSS and the major shifts in our practices as these relate to informational texts, the role of speaking and listening in learning, the development of academic language and vocabulary, and the importance of argumentation in writing. Later in chapter 1, we explain how the standards are organized, so that the thirty-three-page original document and its three appendices become a bit less bewildering. We also discuss what the standards don't say: about English learners, students with disabilities, and those who struggle with literacy. The National Governors Association Center for Best Practices and Council of Chief State School Officers (NGA and CCSSO), developers of the CCSS ELA, provide some general guidelines for students learning English and those who struggle in school, but these are brief summaries and will likely generate a great deal of additional ideas for implementation over the next several years (for more information, visit www.corestandards.org/the-standards for the documents "Application of the Standards for English Language Learners" and "Application to Students With Disabilities"). Importantly, these gaps highlight why PLCs are so important. In the words of the NGA and CCSSO (2010a):

> While the Standards focus on what is most essential, they do not describe all that can or should be taught. A great deal is left to the discretion of teachers and curriculum developers. The aim of the Standards is to articulate the fundamentals, not to set out an exhaustive list or a set of restrictions that limits what can be taught beyond what is specified herein. (p. 6)

Chapters 2, 3, and 4 form the heart of this book because they each focus on a specific *strand* addressed in the CCSS. Reading is the subject of chapter 2: each and every standard is examined as it applies to literary and informational texts, as well as the important reading foundational skills of phonics, word recognition, and fluency that are critical in the development of readers in grades K–2. Chapter 3 turns the spotlight to the Writing standards and similarly reviews each standard as it applies to the major text types students produce: narrative, informational, and persuasive. In chapter 4, we discuss the two sets of Common Core standards that are integral to what we teach and how students learn—through speaking and listening and by understanding and producing academic language and vocabulary.

Chapter 5 returns to the subject of student consideration in the CCSS, including discussion on using formative assessment processes and summative assessment instruments informatively, and designing and implementing interventions for students who are not performing at expected levels.

Know that this book has been designed with you in mind. All of the research cited is specific to grades K–2. In addition, we've designed scenarios written from the perspective of teachers and students in grades K–2 to illuminate the standards.

These scenarios are fictionalized accounts of our personal teaching activities and our collective experience working with teachers across grade levels in schools with diverse populations. We have developed these scenarios as a way to make the ELA standards come alive for you, not just in language arts but also in science, mathematics, and social studies. We want you to personalize this experience as you and your collaborative team plan for implementation of the Common Core for English language arts. To begin this process, we encourage you to reflect on and discuss with your colleagues the following questions.

1. What is the status of collaborative teams at your school? Acknowledging the reality of your school's commitment to an effective PLC process is a critical first step that can establish the future direction for collaborative professional growth. Recall the six characteristics of effective PLCs (pages 1 and 2) and consider the extent to which your PLC embodies these characteristics. If you want to delve deeper into your school's PLC status, you can explore where your school would place on the PLC continuum: preinitiating, initiating, implementing, developing, or sustaining (DuFour et al., 2010). Visit www.allthingsplc.info and search the Tools & Resources section for helpful PLC reproducibles, such as the PLC continuum reproducible "Laying the Foundation" from *Learning by Doing* (DuFour et al., 2010).

2. How are your students performing? Are there areas of need in terms of curriculum development? Are there areas of need in terms of instruction? Are there areas of need in terms of assessment? These questions address key topics for your PLC to consider as you focus on the current status of your school's language arts programs in relation to the expectations of the Common Core

ELA standards. Discussions with your collaborative team will enable you to gain insight into *where you are* and *where you need to go* to support and advance your students' language development.

We've designed this book to guide the conversations that are necessary to fully implement the Common Core State Standards. As such, it should serve as a resource that you return to regularly to consider the ways in which student learning can be improved. The anchor standards and the grade-level expectations define the outcomes expected of us as teachers. *Common Core English Language Arts in a PLC at Work™, Grades K–2* provides the process for you and your collaborative team to achieve those outcomes.

CHAPTER 1

Using Collaborative Teams for English Language Arts

KEY QUESTIONS

- To what extent does your team understand the conceptual shifts represented in the Common Core State Standards for English language arts?

- How often are informational texts used in instruction across the day?

- To what extent do teachers at your school use complex texts?

- Do students routinely discuss and develop texts that feature opinions and evidence?

- To what extent do teachers at your school focus on speaking and listening activities?

- In what ways do teachers at your school develop academic vocabulary and language?

A team of first-grade teachers is meeting to discuss the results of a common formative assessment it had recently administered. Teachers had previously agreed on a pacing guide for their unit focused on informational texts and had discussed the various ways that they would teach the unit. Unlike most previous state standards, the Common Core require an integrated approach to lesson development in which teachers build students' competence in multiple standards simultaneously. As an example, the teachers' three-week unit had its primary focus on the Reading Standards for Informational Text at the first-grade level (RI.1; NGA & CCSSO, 2010a).

- Ask and answer questions about key details in a text. (RI.1.1)

- Describe the connection between two individuals, events, ideas, or pieces of information in a text. (RI.1.3)

- Ask and answer questions to help determine or clarify the meaning of words and phrases in a text. (RI.1.4) (p. 11)

Of course, teachers always have to consider the complexity of text and ensure that students are reading appropriate texts. As part of their common formative assessment, these teachers wanted to determine if students could identify key details from what was explicitly stated in a text and if they could use information from the text to clarify word meanings. They asked students to read a selected passage from *Starfish* (Hurd, 1962) and respond to a number of text-dependent questions, such as "How does a starfish find food?"

The teachers' collaborative discussion about the students' responses to this question centered on how they interpreted the text on p. 17 of the book, which reads:

> It hunts for mussels and oysters
> and clams.
> It feels for the mussels.
> It feels for the oysters.
> It feels for the clams.
> It feels for something to eat.

As Ms. Lopez notes, "Seventy-eight percent of the students got this correct. I'm really impressed with that because I thought that they might answer that they hunt because of the first line on the page."

Agreeing, Ms. Sarmiento adds, "I think that most of our students did really well on this, but I'm also thinking about the 16 percent of students who missed the question and answered that they look for food. The text says that starfish have no eyes, ears, or nose, but I think that the students didn't read for those details or that they didn't make that connection. We might need to think about that group of students for some additional instruction or intervention."

Conversations like this are possible when teachers have the opportunity to work together in collaborative planning teams. To teach the Common Core State Standards well, teachers need to collaborate with their colleagues. In doing so, they can ensure learning for *all* students. It is imperative that collaborative team members work to answer the four critical questions of a PLC as they devote attention to the CCSS (DuFour et al., 2008).

1. What do we want our students to learn?
2. How will we know when they have learned it?
3. How will we respond when some students don't learn?
4. How will we extend and enrich the learning for students who are already proficient?

In other words, teachers need to plan together, look at student work together, identify needs for reteaching together, trust one another, and ask for help when they need it. Figure 1.1 provides a tool that we have found useful in helping collaborative teams work together. As part of their overall PLC work, collaborative teams focus on the four critical questions and begin to build the culture of the school in which student learning drives the discussions teachers and administrators have. Over time, teams will modify and change this form, but to start it is likely useful to focus on each aspect of the tool.

Collaborative Team Meeting Logistics	
Grade:	Date:
Lead teacher or facilitator:	
Teachers in attendance:	

Focus

(Check one.)

☐ Curriculum pacing guide

☐ Strategy implementation

☐ Coaching practice

☐ Consensus scoring cycle

    + Common assessment development

    + Item analysis (See Item Analysis Summary.)

Discussion points:	Questions raised:
Objective for the coming week:	Resources needed:
Implementation steps:	

Item Analysis Summary
Assessment tool:
Areas of strength in student work:
Areas of weakness in student work:
Teacher practice: What should be preserved?
Teacher practice: Identify gaps between existing and desired practice.
Teacher practice: What aspects of existing practice pose a barrier to implementing desired practice?
Teacher practice: Identify interventions or unit modifications.
Unanswered questions:

Source: Adapted from Fisher & Frey, 2007a. Reprinted with permission. Learn more about ASCD at www.ascd.org.

Figure 1.1: Collaborative team meeting record.

Visit **go.solution-tree.com/commoncore** for a reproducible version of this figure.

Over time, teams will modify and change the tool to suit their unique needs, but to start, it is likely useful to focus on each aspect of the tool. At the top of the form ("Collaborative Team Meeting Logistics"), teachers record the grade level, the date of the meeting, who was facilitating, and who was in attendance. Given that there are different phases that a collaborative team uses to complete the work, we ask that the team agree on its focus for each of its collaborative meeting times. Importantly, there may be two or more foci during a meeting, and we ask teams to complete different forms for each shift in focus. The reason for this is simple: the team learns to integrate the stages as a habit of interaction when it names each stage each time. It also provides a record that the team can use to review past efforts to improve student achievement. School systems are very good at documenting when things are going wrong and not so good at recording successes. Using a tool like the one in figure 1.1 provides a record of success that team members can review when they need to revisit a successful time in the past.

The remainder of the logistics portion of the form focuses on the discussion that team members have, including the development of pacing guides, teaching strategy implementation, and peer advice and coaching. During some of the meetings, the team will develop common assessments or review the results of an assessment. We recommend that teams use the "Item Analysis Summary" portion when they are discussing assessment results since there are a number of specific decisions that need to be made in terms of intervention and changes in practice.

Teachers are able to hold these types of conversations because they understand the power of PLCs and the conceptual shifts represented in the Common Core State Standards for English language arts. They also know the specific standards for their grade level and how these are developed across grades K–2. In this chapter, we will discuss these major shifts represented in the CCSS, especially their implications for teaching English language arts. In addition, we will highlight what is *not* included in the standards.

The Common Core State Standards

The adoption of the Common Core State Standards for English language arts extends a trend in U.S. education to collaborate across organizations in order to obtain better learning results. Standards-driven policies and practices have yielded notable results, especially in our collective efforts to articulate purposes and learning outcomes to our stakeholders (Gamoran, 2007). This in turn has led to improved alignment between curriculum, instruction, and assessment. But the years have also exposed weaknesses in the system, many of which are related to the disjointed efforts of individual states trying to put their own standards in motion. No matter how effective the processes or products, states simply could not share them with other states, as no standards were held in common. Consequently, states, like Arkansas and Arizona, could not pool human and fiscal resources to develop common materials and assessments. As standards-based assessments rose to prominence in the 2000s, a mosaic of testing results made it virtually impossible to fairly compare the effectiveness of reform efforts across states.

The National Governors Association Center for Best Practices and Council of Chief State School Officers sought to rectify these shortcomings by sponsoring the development of a shared set of standards each state could agree on. Beginning in 2010, state boards of education began adopting these standards in English language arts and mathematics. In 2012, nearly all the states adopted them and have begun the work of determining timelines for implementation, as well as methods for assessment.

In an effort to capitalize on new opportunities for collaboration among states, two assessment consortia are developing standards-based assessments. Both the Partnership for Assessment of Readiness for College and Careers (PARCC) and the Smarter Balanced Assessment Consortium (SBAC) consist of representatives from states working to develop assessments of the standards. Some states belong to both and will eventually determine which instruments they will use. While these efforts are works in progress, common themes are emerging from both consortia. For one, it is likely that a significant part of the tests will be computer based. In addition, it is anticipated that benchmark assessments will play a prominent role in order for schools to be better able to identify students who are falling behind. But perhaps the biggest shift in these assessments has to do with the ELA standards themselves. (Visit www.parcconline.org or www.smarterbalanced.org for more information.) In the next section, we will outline five major changes to how we view literacy teaching and learning.

Shift One: Focus on Reading and Writing to Inform, Persuade, and Convey Experiences

The Common Core ELA standards reflect a trend in elementary literacy that has been occurring since the 1990s: a deepening appreciation of the importance of informational and persuasive texts in a student's reading diet, or the range of reading genre and materials students encounter across the year. (For now, we will focus our discussion on informational texts, with further attention to persuasive texts featured later in this chapter in the section on argumentation.) The reasons for increasing informational text usage are often related to the need to improve content knowledge (Moss, 2005) to meet increased demand in digital environments (Schmar-Dobler, 2003), and even to prevent the so-called *fourth-grade slump* (Chall & Jacobs, 2003), which suggests that student achievement stagnates in fourth grade. Perhaps reflective of these efforts, access to and use of informational texts appear to be increasing in elementary school. Nell Duke's (2000) study of first-grade classrooms notes that only 3.6 minutes per day are devoted to reading informational texts. Jongseong Jeong, Janet Gaffney, and Jin-Oh Choi's (2010) study of second-, third-, and fourth-grade classrooms' informational text usage finds that while use hovers at one minute per day in the second-grade classrooms, it greatly accelerates to sixteen minutes per day in third- and fourth-grade classrooms. However, this is still well short of Barbara Moss's (2005) measure of informational text usage on standardized tests—50 percent at the fourth-grade level.

In keeping with this data, the CCSS ELA recommend an evenly divided diet of literary and informational texts by the fourth grade (see table 1.1, page 12), gradually increasing throughout middle and high school. Keep in mind that this doesn't mean that students in grades K–2 should no longer be allowed to read narrative text; nothing could be further from the truth. Narrative remains essential as a means of conveying

Table 1.1: Grade Distribution of Literary and Informational Passages in the 2009 NAEP Framework

Grade	Literary Texts	Informational Texts
4	50 percent	50 percent
8	45 percent	55 percent
12	30 percent	70 percent

Source: NGA & CCSSO, 2010a, p. 5.

ideas and concepts through story. However, just as a nutritional diet limited to only one or two foods cannot provide sufficient nourishment, neither should we limit the types of texts used (not just stacked on the bookshelves) in the classroom. As well, it is helpful to measure use of informational texts across the school day, not only in the reading and language arts block, in which teachers use a greater volume of literary texts.

Just as the reading diet of learners needs to be expanded, so does their writing repertoire. A key practice is to link the reading of expository texts with original writing in the same genre, as the link between reading and writing abilities is strong in students (Langer, 1986), and there is an especially strong positive longitudinal effect between grades 2 and 6 (Abbott, Beringer, & Fayol, 2010). Consequently, an effective practice is to link the reading of expository texts to students' original writing of such texts. In other words, consistent exposure to and use of text genres are positively linked to children's growing ability to write within these same genres. In the same way that narrative texts are used as a springboard for young writers to convey their own experiences, informational texts should be used to teach how one explains and persuades.

However, Eliza Beth Littleton (1998) finds that students ages five through nine can be taught to use the oral language rhetorical skills needed to explain and persuade. When purposefully taught, these skills transfer to students' writing ability, and students' capacity to write grows with age and experience.

Notably, Vicki Purcell-Gates, Nell Duke, and Joseph Martineau (2007) examine the science reading and writing experiences of second- and third-grade students to identify effective teaching practices. They discover that explicit teaching of informational writing forms (for example, All About Cats) in science has little effect, while immersion in authentic science reading and writing is strongly correlated to writing ability in this genre. Also, authentic reading and writing immersion coupled with explicit instruction is most effective for science procedural writing (for example, How to Freeze Water Into Ice). In both cases, these effects hold regardless of socioeconomic factors, such as parental educational level.

The ELA standards for grades K–2 call for a major investment in the time teachers spend instructing students to raise their ability to comprehend informational and persuasive texts. This shift may require an assessment of where and when students use these types of texts across the school day. Additionally, there is a renewed expectation that students will also write in these genres. Much of the research on expository writing for grades K–2 students reinforces what many of us already knew: immersion in these texts, when coupled with explicit instruction, can lead to more sophisticated writing (Duke & Roberts, 2010; Moss, 2004).

Shift Two: Focus on Increasing Text Complexity

Closely related to an emphasis on informational texts is "steadily increasing text complexity" (NGA & CCSSO, 2010b, p. 2). This aspect has received considerable attention as educators figure out how to apply a three-part model for determining how complex a reading really is. In addition, U.S. school teams are working to design methods for accessing complex texts among students who struggle to read, English learners, and students with special needs. The CCSS ELA define text complexity as "the inherent difficulty of reading and comprehending a text combined with consideration of reader and task variables; in the Standards, a three-part assessment of text difficulty that pairs qualitative and quantitative measures with reader-task considerations" (NGA & CCSSO, 2010b, p. 43). In other words, it is multidimensional, with attention given to (1) *quantitative* measures, such as readability formulae; (2) *qualitative* factors, such as complexity of ideas, organization, and cohesion; and (3) *reader and task considerations* like motivation and task difficulty.

The issue of text complexity raises the case for backward planning, with the outcome being that graduating high school students are sufficiently prepared to tackle the kinds of texts they will encounter as they enter college and careers. While this may initially seem to be a remote goal for teachers in grades K–2, keeping it in mind is helpful in identifying what texts are useful for students as they move to the intermediate grades.

Appendix B of the Common Core ELA standards (NGA & CCSSO, 2010c), a useful resource for teachers, includes an extensive list of text exemplars to illustrate this concept. These text exemplars should not be misconstrued as a required reading list for a specific grade. To do so would be to ignore the third dimension of identifying complex texts: reader and task considerations. A necessary complication is that the text exemplars are arranged somewhat differently across grade bands due to the developmental nature of reading in elementary school. Text exemplars for grades K–1 and grades 2–3 are listed together. Both lists include stories, poetry, drama, and informational texts that students should read themselves, as well as parallel lists for those that can be used as read-alouds.

Referenced within the standards document is a *staircase* effect to systematically develop students' capacity for understanding more complex texts (NGA & CCSSO, 2010c). This should be considered at several levels of analysis: within a unit of instruction, throughout a school year, and across multiple grades. That is, the texts a student uses at the beginning of a unit to build background knowledge are more explicit, while those that occur later in a unit to deepen student knowledge are less so. Similarly, the texts students utilize early in a given school year are less complex than those that occur near the end. Additionally, students' capacity and stamina for reading complex texts should build across grade-level bands. For this reason, work concerning text complexity should involve at least two collaborative planning team configurations—as teachers work within as well as across grades K–2—to articulate a cohesive plan. These horizontal and vertical team collaborations ensure that students experience a cohesive curriculum without gaps or redundancy.

Text complexity poses a major challenge for educators in grades K–2 as students transition to classroom environments that increasingly rely on texts as a major source of learning. Defining what makes a text complex requires analyzing qualitative factors and quantitative measures, while also considering the characteristics of the reader and the demands of related tasks. In addition, the CCSS encourage teachers to look across units, the school year, and grade bands to build a purposeful plan to staircase student capacity for complex texts.

Shift Three: Focus on Speaking and Listening

Oral language development is widely regarded as a key feature of early elementary education (Roskos, Tabors, & Leinhart, 2009). The research supports for the ELA standards, cited in CCSS appendix A (NGA & CCSSO, 2010b), shed considerable light on the reasons the NGA and CCSSO place such strong emphasis on speaking and listening in the primary grades. The NGA and CCSSO (2010b) state:

> A meta-analysis by Sticht and James (1984) indicates that the importance of oral language extends well beyond the earliest grades. . . . Sticht and James found evidence strongly suggesting that children's listening comprehension outpaces reading comprehension until the middle school years (grades 6–8). (p. 26)

Speaking and listening skills have a concomitant relationship with reading and writing development. To observe this effect, Virginia Berninger and Robert Abbott (2010) examine two cohorts of students from elementary and into middle school, measuring their listening comprehension, speaking expression, reading comprehension, and writing comprehension in grades 1, 3, 5, and 7. They note students' relative strengths and weaknesses vary considerably across the years, supporting the assertion that these language modalities are not fixed, and in fact are influenced considerably by experiences and education. Berninger and Abbott further explain:

> Some [people] still believe that children learn oral language before they come to school and that the purpose of schooling is to teach written language. . . . When the four separate language systems are well integrated and synchronized, language may be experienced as a unitary construct, much as rain is experienced as unitary wetness rather than as isolated drops. (p. 649)

Berninger and Abbott (2010) advocate for a view of "comprehension and expression via language by ear, mouth, hand, and eye" (p. 635), weaving these language experiences into as many instructional events as possible.

The Common Core ELA standards for grades K–2 call for teachers to nest speaking and listening within the context of literacy instruction. Importantly, these performance-based standards include delivering and listening to the presentations of other students and exchanging information and ideas featured in these performance events. Speaking and listening also extend to a variety of instructional arrangements, especially small-group interactions across content areas. Students are encouraged to collaborate with one another and communicate in formal and informal settings; like shifts one and two, they should not be bound exclusively to the reading and language arts block and should be integrated across the school day.

Shift Four: Focus on Text-Based Evidence for Argumentation

A fourth shift concerns the development of argumentation skills. This is unfamiliar to many elementary teachers who typically have experience at rhetorical reading and writing only as college students themselves. Argumentation as a formal process isn't present in the CCSS until grades 6–12. But the foundation for it is built in the primary years through opinion. Importantly, *opinion* doesn't refer to the general definition of the word—after all, everybody has opinions about something—but rather about the academic expectations of opinion. These expectations include stating one's opinion, supporting opinion through evidence and example, and anticipating and addressing opposing opinions. In elementary school, this is demonstrated through persuasive writing and speech.

Although persuasive writing has been featured in most states' content frameworks, it is rarely put into practice in a consistent way (Moore & MacArthur, 2012). A national survey of grades 1–3 teachers finds that little more than 3 percent of them have their students writing opinion pieces—the least common kind of writing done in these classrooms (Cutler & Graham, 2008). The amount of writing alone is inadequate for students to become more skilled at writing persuasively—students do not write enough in school. Additionally, this may have instructional implications as well. Writing is more than just assigning; the skills of writing must be taught as well. In terms of persuasive writing, the complexities are notable.

A second characteristic of persuasion and argumentation is the ability to cite evidence to support one's claims. The use of evidence is at the heart of science instruction. The National Science Education Standards (National Research Council, 1996) require elementary science students to use evidence for argumentation in science discussion and writing. Argumentation skills, like persuasion skills, can be taught. However, they require purposeful instruction and are most often expressed through oral language. In science, we teach students to use language frames in their science discussion, such as "I know that _____ is _____ because _____" and "The reason I believe _____ is _____" (Ross, Fisher, & Frey, 2009). Even among young learners who are not yet writing, developing a habit of *because* encourages them to think closely about evidence. Science is an ideal environment for introducing the concept of argumentation, but these skills can and should be reinforced throughout the school day.

The CCSS ELA encourage the purposeful teaching of developmentally appropriate elements of opinion, argumentation, and persuasion to expand students' breadth and depth of speaking and writing. These rhetorical skills become increasingly essential as students progress to the intermediate grades, with the seeds of logic sown in the primary years. Students gain these skills through reading and writing in small groups and through classroom discourse.

Shift Five: Focus on Academic Vocabulary and Language

A final shift in the Common Core standards concerns the development of academic vocabulary and language. As with the other major conceptual changes, this shift's intent is to foster disciplinary links in order to build learning. This approach acknowledges that vocabulary should not be seen as an isolated list of words but rather as labels that we use as a proxy for conceptual understandings. In fact, the language of the standards illuminates this idea. The CCSS note the use of "general academic and domain-specific words and phrases sufficient for reading, writing, speaking and listening" (NGA & CCSSO, 2010a, p. 25). This underscores two key points: (1) academic vocabulary and language entail the use of a broad range of terms—*lexical dexterity*—and (2) vocabulary development extends beyond teaching decontextualized words (NGA & CCSSO, 2010b).

Much of the research underpinning this view of academic vocabulary and language comes from the work of Isabel Beck, Margaret McKeown, and Linda Kucan (2008), whose familiar three-tier model categorizes words and their instruction.

1. **Tier one:** These words are used in everyday speech, are in the vocabulary of most native speakers, and are taught only in the primary grades. However, students who need more language support, such as English learners, will need instruction beyond the first years of schooling. Examples of tier one words from *Starfish* (Hurd, 1962), the book featured in the chapter opener, include *grows, crawl,* and *hide* (Beck et al., 2008).

2. **Tier two:** These words (called *general academic words and phrases* in the CCSS) appear more often in texts than in verbal exchanges. For instance, *Starfish* (Hurd, 1962) uses *rays, sink, feels, tube,* and *spring*; these are examples of tier two words for first-grade students (Beck et al., 2008). Notice as well that many of these are multiple meaning words, such as *sink, feels,* and *spring*. In addition, they are used in many kinds of texts, not just those that are found within a specific discipline. These need to be explicitly taught throughout the school years.

3. **Tier three:** These words (called *domain-specific words and phrases* in the CCSS) are closely associated with a specific content and also require specific instruction. Examples of such words and phrases in this first-grade informational text include *tide, oysters,* and *snail.*

While teachers often give tier three words and phrases quite a bit of attention, tier two words are more often overlooked. After all, domain-specific words and phrases are closely tied to a discipline and a unit of instruction, and attention is therefore focused on knowing both the definition of the word and its associated concepts. But by overlooking tier two words, students can face more difficulty reading and listening to complex texts because these words "are not unique to a particular discipline . . . are far less well defined by contextual clues . . . and far less likely to be defined explicitly within a text" (NGA & CCSSO, 2010b, p. 33). For example, knowing that a character *scrambled* rather than *ran* alerts the young reader to the character's mood and intent. A *sensible* idea enlightens a student about the way an inventor solved a problem. But unless attention is also provided for these words, readers of complex texts are not able to comprehend at a deeper level. Similarly, students will not use sophisticated terms in their expressive language.

Therefore, an important shift in the standards concerns the importance of using academic language and vocabulary throughout the school day. Special attention should be given to the types of academic language students require in order to express themselves and to understand the writings of others. Furthermore, the rush to profile domain-specific words and phrases can overshadow the importance of general academic vocabulary that students encounter in many kinds of texts. The investment in academic vocabulary and language is well worth it, as vocabulary knowledge is a robust predictor of reading comprehension. Evidence-based instruction, especially for young children who arrive to kindergarten with language deficits, is critical for student success (Jalongo & Sobolak, 2011). Indeed, the size of a child's vocabulary in kindergarten is a strong predictor of reading comprehension in later grades (Scarborough, 2001).

Purposes and Organization of the CCSS ELA

In the previous section, we highlighted five major shifts in the way we look at the literacy development of grades K–2 students across the school day. As noted previously, a primary purpose of the CCSS is to prepare students for eventual college or career choices. All schools aspire to successfully prepare students for the future; however, some argue that starting this in high school is too late for some students (National Education Goals Panel, 1998). However, this doesn't mean that elementary students must start making plans for their adult lives. But insufficient literacy skills do limit one's choices in employment, careers, and postsecondary education. By spotlighting the importance of literacy development across grades K–12, we hope to collectively consider how 21st century instruction factors into students' lives long after they have left our classrooms.

The CCSS spotlight college and career readiness with *anchor standards*. Anchor standards are the threads that tie the grade-level standards together, whether in kindergarten or senior year. Anchor standards frame each language strand: Reading, Writing, Speaking and Listening, and Language.

Figure 1.2 explains the different elements of the Common Core State Standards for English language arts.

Strands are the categories for English language arts in K–5 and 6–12: Reading, Writing, Speaking and Listening, and Language. Additionally, literacy in history and social studies, science, and technical subjects in grades 6–12 focuses on two strands—Reading and Writing.

College and career readiness (CCR) anchor standards define general, cross-disciplinary expectations for reading, writing, speaking and listening, and language. These anchor standards are designated by strand and standard number; for example, R.CCR.6 signifies reading strand (R), anchor standard (CCR), and standard number (six). This standard is from the domain Craft and Structure, which has three standards numbered four, five, and six. The anchor standards are numbered consecutively, one through ten, in the domains.

Domains define categories of CCR anchor standards for each of the strands in the CCSS ELA—Reading, Writing, Speaking and Listening, and Language. For example, four domains are defined for the Writing strand: Text Types and Purposes (standards one, two, and three), Production and Distribution of Writing (standards four, five, and six), Research to Build and Present Knowledge (standards seven, eight, and nine), and Range of Writing (standard ten).

Grade-specific standards define what students should understand and be able to do. The grade-specific standards parallel the CCR anchor standards by translating the broader CCR statements into grade-appropriate end-of-year expectations.

Grade-specific standards are designated by strand, anchor standard, grade level, and standard number; for example, RL.K.1 signifies Reading Standards for Literature (RL), kindergarten level (K), and standard one in the domain Key Ideas and Details.

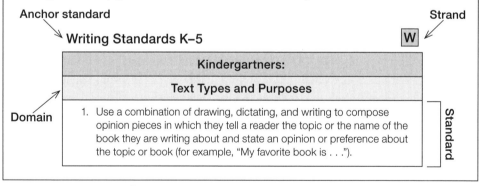

Source: Adapted from NGA & CCSSO, 2010a, p. 19.

Figure 1.2: How to read the CCSS ELA.

In the next three chapters, we utilize the anchor standards as a means for fostering the work of collaborative planning teams. The following principles for college and career readiness shape these anchor standards and describe the growing capabilities of learners as they progress through school. To be college and career ready, students must do the following.

- **Demonstrate independence:** Students must comprehend complex texts in all content areas, participate as speakers and listeners in academic discussions and presentations, direct their own learning, and utilize resources.

- **Build strong content knowledge across all subjects and disciplines:** Cross-discipline knowledge is important for students' writing and discussions. In addition, students should engage in the research and study skills needed to build their content knowledge.

- **Respond to the varying demands of audience, task, purpose, and discipline:** College- and career-ready students communicate in speaking and writing with a range of audiences and are knowledgeable about the variances of discipline-specific evidence.

- **Comprehend as well as critique:** Students learn this skill as they read and listen to others. They are able to ask questions, evaluate information, and discern reasonableness.

- **Value evidence:** Students should provide evidence in their own oral and written discourse and expect others to furnish evidence.

- **Use technology and digital media strategically and capably:** As they integrate online and offline resources, students should use critical-thinking and communication skills within their digital lives.

- **Understand other perspectives and cultures:** In order to better communicate with and learn from and alongside people, students should understand a wide range of cultural and experiential backgrounds.

The principles and assumptions that guided development of the anchor standards provide a framework for understanding them and their function in girding the grade-level standards. While the CCSS map the territory for literacy development, it does not pretend to describe every aspect of teaching and learning.

What Is Not Covered in the Standards

Keep in mind that the standards themselves are end-point results. It has been left to educators, instructional leaders, and curriculum developers to design the ways to get there. The CCSS state, "The Standards define what all students are expected to know and be able to do, not how teachers should teach" (NGA & CCSSO, 2010a, p. 6). This is intentional, as it is essential for educators at the local, state, and national levels to engage in dialogue about essential topics related to content and scope, intervention methods and materials, and supports and expectations for English learners, students with special needs, and students who struggle.

The Content and Scope

The Common Core ELA standards describe essential outcomes but do not address all aspects of learning, or even disciplines, that are important for learners. The authors use *play* as an example, acknowledging that it is critical in the learning lives of young children but is not featured in the standards themselves (NGA & CCSSO, 2010a). Even within the scope of the English language arts, not all aspects are featured. For instance, handwriting is not mentioned, even though every primary teacher devotes time to this endeavor. Consequently, some states have supplemented the standards with additional content. For example, California added an expectation about following multistep directions in the K–2 Speaking and Listening standards (California State Department of Education, n.d.; Sacramento County Office of Education, 2012). The Common Core State Standards are intended to guide the development of formative and summative assessments. It is important for states to cap their additions to ensure they do not undermine this design and make it impossible to develop meaningful assessments that can be used across states. This process will ensure that assessment results based on the CCSS will allow for comparisons of student performance across states. PARCC and SBAC, the two consortia developing standards-based assessments, consist of representatives from states that provide additional opportunities for collaboration among states. Teachers should check their state's department of education website to determine any content that's been added to the CCSS.

The concept of *play* bears further discussion, as it is crucial in the discussion of young children's learning development. To be sure, play helps a child develop the social skills he or she will need to be successful in an environment filled with other children. Critical skills such as taking turns, delaying gratification, and handling disappointment are fostered through meaningful interactions with others. In addition, children exhibit early literacy behaviors through play (Harste, Woodward, & Burke, 1984). These behaviors include exploring materials together, writing messages, and "using language, other symbolic expressions, and artifacts, of thinking, feeling, believing, valuing, and acting that can be used to identify oneself as a member" among a group of people (Gee, 1996, p. 131). An adult may simply see young children pretending to be superheroes or wild animals; a primary educator understands that students create oral texts through play and express their understanding of print in this way. While the CCSS stress the academic nature of school expectations, developmentally appropriate practices involving play make it possible for young children to reach them.

Intervention Methods and Materials

The standards should be viewed as end-of-grade expectations, but they do not in any way describe either the approaches for intervention or the materials used to accompany them. In every school, some students are performing well below grade-level expectations, and some are currently benefitting from a response to intervention (RTI) approach to learning. RTI involves identifying whether, and to what extent, a struggling student is responding positively to intervention that has been designed to meet the individual learner's needs.

His or her responsiveness (or unresponsiveness) to intervention is determined through dynamic, ongoing assessment that monitors student progress and shapes modifications to the assessment plan. The CCSS ELA do not discuss RTI; however, we will explore this topic in chapter 5.

Supports and Expectations for English Learners

The NGA and CCSSO include people knowledgeable about issues related to English learners. NGA and CCSSO acknowledge that students acquiring English require supports and that these supports should be carefully designed to meet the needs of these students (see "Application of Common Core State Standards for English Language Learners," www .corestandards.org/assets/application-for-english-learners.pdf). They caution, however, that accommodations should not result in a reduction of expectations for fear that the trajectory of these students' educational progress will be severely compromised.

Supports and Expectations for Students With Special Needs

Similarly, the CCSS do not define supports for students with special needs beyond assistive technologies such as Braille, screen-reader technologies, sign language, and so on. Use of such devices is determined through an individual education program (IEP) and supersedes educational standards. These devices and approaches are more commonly used for students with sensory or motor disabilities, or in some cases, for those with mild disabilities that involve reading and learning (see "Application to Students With Disabilities," www.corestandards.org/assets/application-to-students-with-disabilities .pdf). What has not been determined is how these supports and expectations might be adapted for students with more significant cognitive and intellectual delays and disabilities. It is likely that development of these systems will continue as general and special educators collaborate. Participation and access are priorities, and the CCSS language mirrors that used in the Individuals With Disabilities Education Improvement Act of 2004 (http://idea.ed.gov): "The Standards should also be read as allowing for the widest possible range of students to participate fully from the outset and as permitting appropriate accommodations to ensure maximum participation of students with special education needs" (NGA & CCSSO, 2010a, p. 6).

Supports and Expectations for Students Who Struggle

The CCSS do not provide specific advice about supporting students who struggle with school. Instead, there is a recognition that expectations are often reduced and students fail to reach high levels of achievement. Support for students who struggle with school should be part of the ongoing conversations within collaborative planning teams. As Richard DuFour, Rebecca DuFour, and Robert Eaker (2008) note, collaborative teams should discuss what to do when students fail to achieve the expected learning targets. During discussions, team members can identify additional instructional interventions to close the gap between students who mastered the content and those who did not. This may involve reteaching content through guided instruction or targeting students for RTI efforts (Fisher & Frey, 2010). A pyramid of RTI that provides teams with systems for intervention can be helpful (Buffum, Mattos, & Weber, 2008). In this book, we focus on quality teaching for all students and encourage the development of collaborative planning teams to monitor and adapt instruction to ensure learning for all students. This systematic approach to students who struggle in school has a better potential to result in positive outcomes than reducing expectations or preventing students from accessing high-quality instruction aligned with the Common Core State Standards. That's not to say that teachers should avoid scaffolding or support. As we will discuss in each of the teaching scenarios in this book, teaching Common Core ELA well requires a deep understanding of the content as well as skills in responding to students' understanding and misunderstanding.

Conclusion

The Common Core State Standards for English language arts present K–2 educators with challenges as well as opportunities. The shifts in our ways of thinking about literacy development are considerable and require us to collectively look at our own practices and plan collaboratively with our colleagues. These can pose a major roadblock for schools that do not have a forum for conducting this important work. It is not the kind of work that can be accomplished in a few workshops and some follow-up meetings. Determining how these changes will be implemented, as well as identifying the effective practices that have already proven to be successful, will require focused and sustained attention as educators develop curriculum, design formative assessments, and interpret results. Collaborative teams within a professional learning community are an ideal forum for accomplishing this work. Indeed, the major shifts described in this chapter parallel the characteristics of successful professional learning communities: they emphasize collaboration and communication across disciplines and grade levels, and they reward those who seek to deepen their understanding of their professional practice.

CHAPTER 2

Implementing the Common Core State Standards for Reading

KEY QUESTIONS

- To what extent does your team understand the Reading standards: What is familiar? What is new? What may be challenging for students? What may be challenging for teachers?

- Examine current texts being used in grades K–2 and assess them qualitatively and for reader and task demands. Which ones work? Which ones should be used in another grade or eliminated altogether?

- How do K–2 teachers at your school teach the foundational reading skills?

Tom Allen's kindergarten students are learning about transportation and text structures. Mr. Allen introduces *Truck* (Crews, 1980), a *wordless* book that describes a truck as it travels from a loading dock through the city to make a delivery of bicycles. Some words are included as part of the illustrations. However, words are not used to provide the main information of the text. Mr. Allen is using this informational text to develop his students' understanding of text structure and beginning, middle, and end. The students must use their visual analysis skills, as the illustrations are crucial to detecting the story structure. "It is giving me a great way to introduce a sequence of events, before they even realize it. I want them to develop their understanding that things occur in a specific order," Mr. Allen says.

In addition to building knowledge of text structure and chronological order, the class is also learning how to analyze an informational text. "Many of the informational texts the students read provide explicit information, while others require the reader to infer," Mr. Allen explains. "Our grade-level team also wants to give students experience reading a wide variety of informational texts."

On the first day of this unit, the class discusses the purpose of the book and the information on each page. For example, one page features an illustration of a bus coming out of a tunnel and the truck going into a tunnel. As part of the discussion, Arturo comments, "This is the back of the truck, so it means it goes in that way." Brandi adds, "The bus goes this way [*pointing in the opposite direction of the truck*]."

Over the course of a week, the class looks at the pictures and discusses the text at length. "I start each lesson after day one by having the students retell the contents of the text to their partner while I listen in on their discussions," Mr. Allen says. "I remind them to tell the events in order, and we have practiced using the words *beginning*, *middle*, and *end*. We also talk in greater detail about different pages, adding to the students' vocabulary knowledge. For example, I overheard Marco saying, 'First, the truck got filled up with bikes. That's at the beginning. In the middle, the truck drives down a road in the rain. It goes over the bridge. That bridge is in the fog. And at the end, the truck is empty except for one bike'." Mr. Allen is pleased with his students' progress and plans to discuss their developing mastery of three of the Reading Standards for Informational Text (RI.K) (NGA & CCSSO, 2010a, p. 13) with his collaborative team. These standards are:

- With prompting and support, ask and answer questions about key details in a text. (RI.K.1)

- With prompting and support, describe the connection between two individuals, events, ideas, or pieces of information in a text. (RI.K.3)

- With prompting and support, describe the relationship between illustrations and the text in which they appear. (RI.K.7)

A Collaborative Planning Team in Action

Before delving into the main purpose of this chapter, which is to examine the Common Core State Standards for reading in grades K–2, we want to comment on Mr. Allen's curricular decisions and the contributions of his collaborative planning team toward this effort.

Working together, Mr. Allen and his collaborative team developed a consistent and coherent approach for planning the instructional units by taking the following actions.

- Examining the text exemplars in appendix B of the CCSS (NGA & CCSSO, 2010c) to gain a sense of the text complexity appropriate for kindergarten students

- Identifying texts they currently use to teach students how to compare and contrast

- Creating a list identifying a range of informational texts and literature readings that represented a progression of complexity throughout the school year

- Matching identified texts to concepts and content to be taught in kindergarten, including in mathematics, social studies, science, and the visual and performing arts

- Developing lessons to be delivered and common formative assessments to be administered

- Discussing findings with one another during their weekly meetings to plan interventions for students in need of extra supports, including those who struggle to read and comprehend grade-level texts

- Developing a classroom observation schedule so they could spend time in one another's classrooms

In other words, Mr. Allen didn't work alone to develop and teach this unit. He relied on the collective strengths of his team to develop the unit and analyze student outcomes. However, before the team could engage in these actions, members had to analyze the Common Core ELA standards and compare these to their existing curriculum and instruction. They used four questions to guide their analysis.

1. What is familiar in the CCSS at each grade level?

2. What appears to be new based on prior standards?

3. What may be challenging for students?

4. What may be challenging for teachers?

This initial conversation allowed this teacher team to begin an analysis of its current status in curriculum and instruction. Importantly, the teachers also included student learning from the outset. Based on its initial work, the team was able to identify areas of need regarding professional development and materials acquisition and set the stage for later decisions regarding curriculum development, data analysis, intervention, and collaborative observations. Figure 2.1 (page 26) shows the initial tool Mr. Allen's collaborative planning team used in its analysis. Visit **go.solution-tree.com/commoncore** for an online-only reproducible of figure 2.1, which your collaborative team can use to analyze other reading standards.

Anchor Standards for Reading

The Common Core English language arts standards are organized across four *strands*: Reading, Writing, Speaking and Listening, and Language. As discussed in chapter 1, a set of K–12 anchor standards for college and career readiness frames each strand. These anchor standards articulate the overarching goals that shape the grade-specific standards and are designed to create commonality across elementary, middle, and high school. "Students advancing through the grades are expected to meet each year's grade-specific standards and retain or further develop skills and understandings mastered in preceding grades" (NGA & CCSSO, 2010a, p. 11). This structure can reduce the *silo effect* that can creep into education in which teachers work in isolation from their peers and curriculum is not coordinated. By viewing education across grade bands and buildings, we can begin to mirror more closely the experiences of our students and their families. The anchor standards are an attempt to foster communication across and within educational systems.

Reading anchor standard five (R.CCR.5): Analyze the structure of texts, including how specific sentences, paragraphs, and larger portions of the text (a section, chapter, scene, or stanza) relate to each other and the whole.

CCSS grade band: Grades K–2

CCSS strand: Reading Standards for Informational Text (RI)

Anchor standard domain: Craft and Structure

Grade-Level Standard	What Is Familiar?	What Is New?	What May Be Challenging for Students?	What May Be Challenging for Teachers?
Kindergarten **RI.K.5:** Identify the front cover, back cover, and title page of a book.				
Grade 1 **RI.1.5:** Know and use various text features (such as headings, tables of contents, glossaries, electronic menus, and icons) to locate key factors or information in a text.				
Grade 2 **RI.2.5:** Know and use various text features (such as captions, bold print, subheadings, glossaries, indexes, electronic menus, and icons) to locate key facts or information in a text efficiently.				

Source: Adapted from NGA & CCSSO, 2010a, p. 13.

Figure 2.1: Guiding questions for grade-by-grade analysis of the Reading standards.

Visit **go.solution-tree.com/commoncore** for a reproducible version of this figure.

There are ten K–5 anchor standards for reading organized into the following four domains (NGA & CCSSO, 2010a, p. 10).

1. Key Ideas and Details

2. Craft and Structure

3. Integration of Knowledge and Ideas

4. Range of Reading and Level of Text Complexity

These anchor standards are directly tied to two parts within the Reading strand at grades K–12: (1) Literature and (2) Informational Text. A third part, Foundational Skills, is specific to K–5 only; it is the only one that does not have a set of anchor standards. We will examine each of these in this chapter, after first discussing the anchor standards in more detail.

Key Ideas and Details

The first three anchor standards describe the explicit and implicit comprehension of readers as they glean the purposes and main points of the text. In addition, the domain emphasizes the importance of being able to follow plot, character development, and themes, all necessary for literary analysis.

1. Read closely to determine what the text says explicitly and to make logical inferences from it; cite specific textual evidence when writing or speaking to support conclusions drawn from the text. (R.CCR.1)

2. Determine central ideas or themes of a text and analyze their development; summarize the key supporting details and ideas. (R.CCR.2)

3. Analyze how and why individuals, events, and ideas develop and interact over the course of a text. (R.CCR.3) (NGA & CCSSO, 2010a, p. 10)

Craft and Structure

The three anchor standards in this domain discuss the reader's ability to analyze texts at the micro and macro levels. Readers should attend to the author's craft in how he or she purposefully uses word choice, literary techniques, and organizational structures to shape the text, a character's voice and experiences, or the interaction between the choice of genre and the information shared.

4. Interpret words and phrases as they are used in a text, including determining technical, connotative, and figurative meanings, and analyze how specific word choices shape meaning or tone. (R.CCR.4)

5. Analyze the structure of texts, including how specific sentences, paragraphs, and larger portions of the text (e.g., a section, chapter, scene, or stanza) relate to each other and the whole. (R.CCR.5)

6. Assess how point of view or purpose shapes the content and style of a text. (R.CCR.6) (NGA & CCSSO, 2010a, p. 10)

Integration of Knowledge and Ideas

In this domain, anchor standards seven through nine are dedicated to the content within and across texts, in print, and in digital environments. Anchor standard seven (R.CCR.7) is also closely tied to a Writing anchor standard domain Research to Build and Present Knowledge (see NGA & CCSSO, 2010a, p. 21), as well as the Speaking and Listening anchor standard domain Comprehension and Collaboration (see NGA & CCSSO, 2010a, p. 24). Anchor standard eight (R.CCR.8) on argumentation is not addressed in the Literature part of the Reading strand as it is not applicable to these text types.

7. Integrate and evaluate content presented in diverse media and formats, including visually and quantitatively, as well as in words. (R.CCR.7)

8. Delineate and evaluate the argument and specific claims in a text, including the validity of the reasoning as well as the relevance and sufficiency of the evidence. (R.CCR.8)

9. Analyze how two or more texts address similar themes or topics in order to build knowledge or to compare the approaches the authors take. (R.CCR.9) (NGA & CCSSO, 2010a, p. 10)

Range of Reading and Level of Text Complexity

This domain with the tenth and final anchor standard for reading has arguably been the predominant topic of discussion about the CCSS ELA.

10. Read and comprehend complex literary and informational texts independently and proficiently. (R.CCR.10) (NGA & CCSSO, 2010a, p. 10)

The Common Core ELA and its appendices devote a considerable amount of space to this standard, noting that students' use of complex texts has diminished since the 1970s, while texts used in college and the workplace have not (Chall, Conard, & Harris, 1977; Hayes, Wolfer, & Wolfe, 1996; as cited in NGA & CCSSO, 2010b). The CCSS advocate for a staircase approach to systematically raising reading comprehension and critical thinking through the purposeful use of complex texts that require students to stretch their cognitive and metacognitive abilities (NGA & CCSSO, 2010a). For students who struggle with reading, this means that they must be taught with complex texts and asked to read increasingly complex texts across the year. However, it is important to note that the text alone should not be the only scaffold; instruction is critical for these students to progress and accelerate.

Text complexity is defined across three dimensions: (1) quantitative measures, (2) qualitative factors, and (3) reader and task considerations. Quantitative measures, using a mixture of word length, sentence length, and syllables, are familiar to elementary educators. In addition, many readability formulae calculate the number of difficult words that appear in a text by comparing these to grade-level lists. Examples of quantitative measures include the Fry Readability Formula, Dale-Chall Readability Formula, and Flesch-Kincaid Grade-Level Index (see Fisher, Frey, & Lapp, 2012), as well as commercial ones such as ATOS (used by Accelerated Reader), Source Rater (Educational Testing

Service), Pearson Reading Maturity Scale (Pearson Education), Degrees of Reading Power (Questar), and Lexile (MetaMetrics). Table 2.1 compares these readability scales. Published quantitative reading scores can provide a platform for collaborative teams to begin to examine which texts to use with their students.

Table 2.1: Text Complexity Ranges Within Grade Bands

Grade Band	Revised CCSS 2011	Accelerated Reader	Degrees of Reading Power	Flesch-Kincaid	Source Rater	Reading Maturity Scale
K–1	n/a	n/a	n/a	n/a	n/a	n/a
2–3	420–820	2.75–5.14	42–54	1.98–5.34	0.05–2.48	3.53–6.13
4–5	740–1010	4.97–7.03	52–60	4.51–7.73	0.84–5.75	5.42–7.92
6–8	925–1185	7.00–9.98	57–67	6.51–10.34	4.11–10.66	7.04–9.57
9–10	1050–1335	9.67–12.01	62–72	8.32–12.12	9.02–13.93	8.41–10.81
11–CCR	1185–1385	11.20–14.10	67–74	10.34–14.20	12.30–14.50	9.57–12.00

Source: CCSSO, 2012.

Importantly, these quantitative measures are not commonly used in kindergarten and grade 1, as noted in the figure. The texts commonly used in primary-grade classrooms do not lend themselves to quantitative analysis. Also, note that the CCSS measures are revised; consequently, these measures differ from those provided in the Common Core ELA. For example, the original range for the grades 2–3 band was 450–725L compared to the revised range of 420–820L (NGA & CCSSO, 2010b, p. 8). Lexile measures are based on word frequency (semantic difficulty) and sentence (length), both of which have been shown to be effective predictors of text difficulty (Lennon & Burdick, 2004).

Computers use mathematical formulae to estimate difficulty. Teachers and parents focus on ideas that will confuse the reader or be inappropriate for students at a given age. Furthermore, teachers use their knowledge of text structures to identity areas of difficulty that will require instruction.

Qualitative factors of texts include the following (Fisher et al., 2012; NGA & CCSSO, 2010b).

- **Levels of meaning or purpose:** Such as the density and complexity of the information, use of figurative language, and stated and implied purposes

- **Structure:** Including the text's genre, organization, narration, and use of text features and graphics

- **Language conventionality and clarity:** Especially in its use of English language variations and registers

- **Knowledge demands:** Including the assumed background knowledge, prior knowledge, cultural knowledge, and vocabulary knowledge

Qualitative factors can make a text more or less complex, and they cannot be measured quantitatively. For instance, the book *Raising Sweetness* (Stanley, 1999) has a Lexile scale score of 530L, situating it near the lower end of the 2–3 grade band. But the text's extensive use of the southwestern U.S. cowboy dialect makes this much more difficult for some readers to understand. In addition, the book requires extensive cultural knowledge about cowboys and the Old West. Assessment of text complexity using these factors is an excellent task for members of a collaborative team who are experienced with using a text and are familiar with a specific text's structure.

Using the rubric in table 2.2 (pages 31–33), a second-grade team meets to discuss informational texts for use in their classrooms. The team members turn their attention to *From Seed to Plant* (Gibbons, 1991a), an informational text with a Lexile score of 660L. The team identifies several aspects of the book that would make it more or less difficult for students. The teachers note that the book has a straightforward purpose, a factor that makes the text more understandable. In addition, text features—like illustrations and diagrams—reinforce narration information. The team agrees that vocabulary makes the book more complex. The teachers also recognize that the density of information also contributes to the text complexity. Mr. Allen notes, "There's so much to remember in this text. It's full of great details, but that makes it much more complex." By identifying what makes the text more complex, the team is able to design instruction around reading dense text, identifying target vocabulary, and taking notes based on the information.

The third dimension for determining text complexity concerns the match between the reader and the task (NGA & CCSSO, 2010b). Factors that are internal to the reader include his or her cognitive capabilities, motivation, knowledge, and experiences. The task demand also influences the relative difficulty of the text. Teacher-led tasks, such as an interactive read-aloud, provide a high degree of scaffolding and make an otherwise difficult text much more comprehensible. Peer-led tasks, such as a small-group text discussion, provide a moderate level of scaffolding as students collaborate to understand the task. Individual tasks, such as independent reading, provide the least amount of scaffolding and place most of the responsibility on the reader's shoulders. In order for students to progress toward increasingly more complex texts, they need a mixture of all of these tasks (Fisher et al., 2012). An over-reliance on one level of task difficulty occurs at the expense of others and can stymie a student's progress. This is perhaps the ongoing discussion collaborative planning teams should have as they design instruction with specific students in mind.

While the anchor standards for reading ground the grade-level standards, there is some overlap in grade levels as it pertains to text exemplars. You may recall that the exemplars are organized somewhat differently to reflect the developmental nature of reading. Therefore, the text exemplars are categories across K–1, with a separate list for grades 2–3 (NGA & CCSSO, 2010c). Because of this, it is wise for teachers to devote some time to discussing text complexity with their colleagues in other grades. This will ensure agreement about texts considered appropriate for the lower end of the grade band (for example, second grade) and the higher level of the grade band (for example, third grade).

Table 2.2: Qualitative Measures of Text Complexity

	3 Points (Stretch) Texts That Stretch a Reader or Require Instruction	2 Points (Grade Level) Texts That Require Grade-Appropriate Skills	1 Point (Comfortable) Texts That Are Comfortable or Build Background, Fluency, and Skills
	Levels of Meaning and Purpose		
Density and Complexity	Text has significant density and complexity, with multiple levels of meaning; meanings may be more ambiguous.	Text has a single, but more complex or abstract level of meaning; some meanings are stated, while others are left to the reader to identify.	Text has single and literal levels of meaning; meaning is explicitly stated.
Figurative Language	Figurative language plays a significant role in identifying the meaning of the text; more sophisticated figurative language is used (irony and satire, allusions, archaic or less familiar symbolism); the reader is left to interpret these meanings.	Figurative language such as imagery, metaphors, symbolism, and personification are used to make connections within the text to more explicit information, and readers are supported in understanding these language devices through examples and explanations.	There is a limited use of symbolism, metaphors, and poetic language that allude to other unstated concepts; language is explicit and relies on literal interpretations.
Purpose	The purpose is deliberately withheld from the reader, who must use other interpretative skills to identify it.	The purpose is implied but is easily identified based on title or context.	The purpose or main idea is directly and explicitly stated at the beginning of the reading.
	Structure		
Genre	Genre is unfamiliar or bends and expands the rules for the genre.	Genre is either unfamiliar but is a reasonable example or it is a familiar genre that bends and expands the rules for the genre.	Genre is familiar, and the text is consistent with the elements of that genre.

continued →

	3 Points (Stretch) — Texts That Stretch a Reader or Require Instruction	2 Points (Grade Level) — Texts That Require Grade-Appropriate Skills	1 Point (Comfortable) — Texts That Are Comfortable or Build Background, Fluency, and Skills
Structure			
Organization	The organization distorts time or sequence in a deliberate effort to delay the reader's full understanding of the plot, process, or set of concepts; may include significant flashbacks, foreshadowing, or shifting perspectives.	The organization adheres to most conventions, but digresses on occasion to temporarily shift the reader's focus to another point of view, event, time, or place, before returning to the main idea or topic.	The organization is conventional, sequential, or chronological, with clear signals and transitions to lead the reader through a story, process, or set of concepts.
Narration	An unreliable narrator provides a distorted or limited view to the reader; the reader must use other clues to deduce the truth; multiple narrators provide conflicting information; shifting points of view keep the reader guessing.	Third-person limited or first-person narration provides accurate, but limited perspectives or viewpoints.	Third-person omniscient narration or an authoritative and credible voice provides an appropriate level of detail and keeps little hidden from the view of the reader.
Text Features and Graphics	There is limited use of text features to organize information and guide the reader. Information in the graphics is not repeated in the main part of the text but is essential for understanding the text.	Has a wider array of text features including margin notes, diagrams, graphs, font changes, and other devices that compete for the reader's attention; graphics and visuals are used to augment and illustrate information in the main part of the text.	Text features (such as bold and italicized words, headings, and subheadings) organize information explicitly and guide the reader; graphics or illustrations may be present but are not necessary to understand the main part of the text.
Language Conventionality and Clarity			
Standard English and Variations	The text includes significant and multiple styles of English and its variations, and these are unfamiliar to the reader.	Some distance exists between the reader's linguistic base and the language conventions used in the text; the vernacular used is unfamiliar to the reader.	The language closely adheres to the reader's linguistic base.

Knowledge Demands

Register	The register is archaic, formal, domain specific, or scholarly.	The register is consultative or formal, and may be academic but acknowledges the developmental level of the reader.	The register is casual and familiar.
Background Knowledge	The text places demands on the reader that extend far beyond his or her experiences, and provides little in the way of explanation of these divergent experiences.	There is distance between the reader's experiences and those in the text, but there is acknowledgement of these divergent experiences, and sufficient explanation to bridge the gaps.	The text contains content that closely matches the reader's life experiences.
Prior Knowledge	Presumes specialized or technical content knowledge, and little in the way of review or explanation of these concepts is present in the text.	Requires subject-specific knowledge, but the text augments this with review or summary of this information.	The prior knowledge needed to understand the text is familiar, and it draws on a solid foundation of practical, general, and academic learning.
Cultural Knowledge	The text relies on extensive or unfamiliar intertextuality and uses artifacts and symbols that reference archaic or historical cultures.	The text primarily references contemporary and popular culture to anchor explanations for new knowledge; intertextuality is used more extensively but is mostly familiar to the reader.	The reader uses familiar cultural templates to understand the text with limited or familiar intertextuality.
Vocabulary Knowledge	Vocabulary demand is extensive, domain specific, and representative of complex ideas; the text offers little in the way of context clues to support the reader.	Vocabulary draws on domain specific, general academic, and multiple meaning words, with text supports to guide the reader's correct interpretations of meanings; the vocabulary represents familiar concepts and ideas.	Vocabulary is controlled and uses the most commonly held meanings; multiple meaning words are used in a limited fashion.

Source: Adapted from Fisher et al., 2012.

Visit go.solution-tree.com/commoncore for a reproducible version of this table.

The anchor standards, and the grade-level standards that follow them, are far too complex to teach in a single lesson or to teach in isolation. Keeping this concept in mind is important as collaborative team members examine these standards for in-depth reading. It is the interaction of these standards within and across domains that makes them powerful. To divide and then reassemble them as isolated lessons will undermine the enduring understandings the standards articulate. The overarching goal should be to teach the habits of effective communicators and to avoid isolated strategy instruction (Frey, Fisher, & Berkin, 2008).

In the following sections, we will examine the Reading strand's parts—Literature, Informational Text, and Foundational Skills—across K–2. This grade band is an essential vantage point for viewing and discussing the CCSS, precisely because it prevents the silo effect that can occur when grade-level teachers operate independently from one another. While grade-level planning must occur, the work of the PLC should first and foremost foster communication and collaboration across grades in order to maximize the potential that the anchor standards afford.

Reading Standards for Literature in Grades K–2

Literature is linked directly to narrative text types—poems, drama, and stories, including folktales, fantasy, and realistic fiction. Although nonfiction biographies and autobiographies often use a narrative structure, they are situated as a type of informational text. Students in the primary grades are traditionally exposed to a high volume of literature, although genres like poetry and folktales are often reserved for specific genre studies units and used more rarely across the school year. Table 2.3 contains sample titles from the text exemplars in appendix B of the Common Core State Standards (NGA & CCSSO, 2010c).

Table 2.3: Exemplars for Literature Texts in Grades K–2

Genre	Kindergarten	Grade 1	Grade 2
Stories	Arnold (2005): *Hi! Fly Guy*	Lobel (1999): *Frog and Toad Together*	Steig (1971): *Amos and Boris*
Poetry	Rossetti (1893): "Mix a Pancake"	Giovanni (1980): "Covers"	Soto (1995): "Eating While Reading"
Read-Aloud Stories	Henkes (2004): *Kitten's First Full Moon*	Garza (2005): *Family Pictures/Cuadros de Familia*	Say (2000): *The Sign Painter*
Read-Aloud Poetry	Langstaff (1992): *Over in the Meadow*	Moss (2000): *Zin! Zin! Zin! A Violin*	Fleischman (1989): "Fireflies"

Source: Adapted from NGA & CCSSO, 2010c.

The standards for literature for each grade level are drawn directly from the anchor standards and are organized in the same manner: Key Ideas and Details, Craft and

Structure, Integration of Knowledge and Ideas, and Range of Reading and Level of Text Complexity. We invite you and your collaborative team to discuss the standards using the four-part protocol described in figure 2.1 (page 26): (1) What is familiar? (2) What is new? (3) What may be challenging for students? (4) What may be challenging for teachers? (Visit **go.solution-tree.com/commoncore** for an online-only reproducible you can use to conduct analyses of other standards with your collaborative team.) We will share our observations to seed your discussions.

Key Ideas and Details in Literature

Table 2.4 shows the K–2 standards for this domain. The standards contain many expected elements, as well as some more challenging demands that have implications for instruction.

Table 2.4: Literature Standards for Domain Key Ideas and Details, Grades K–2

Anchor Standards	Kindergarten Standards	Grade 1 Standards	Grade 2 Standards
R.CCR.1: Read closely to determine what the text says explicitly and to make logical inferences from it; cite specific textual evidence when writing or speaking to support conclusions drawn from the text.	**RL.K.1:** With prompting and support, ask and answer questions about key details in a text.	**RL.1.1:** Ask and answer questions about key details in a text.	**RL.2.1:** Ask and answer such questions as who, what, where, when, why, and how to demonstrate understanding of key details of a text.
R.CCR.2: Determine central ideas or themes of a text and analyze their development; summarize the key supporting details and ideas.	**RL.K.2:** With prompting and support, retell familiar stories, including key details.	**RL.1.2:** Retell stories, including key details, and demonstrate understanding of their central message or lesson.	**RL.2.2:** Recount stories, including fables and folktales from diverse cultures, and determine their central message, lesson, or moral.
R.CCR.3: Analyze how and why individuals, events, and ideas develop and interact over the course of a text.	**RL.K.3:** With prompting and support, identify characters, settings, and major events in a story.	**RL.1.3:** Describe characters, settings, and major events in a story, using key details.	**RL.2.3:** Describe how characters in a story respond to major events and challenges.

Source: Adapted from NGA & CCSSO, 2010a, pp. 10 and 11.

Anchor standard two (R.CCR.2) highlights the importance of being able to recount stories including key details and eventually adding specific genres and central messages, with an expectation that this will be further developed in the upper grades. This is linked to the expectations for anchor standard three (R.CCR.3) that students are able to identify characters, settings, and major events. As they grow, students develop their understanding of story elements, such as character and setting, and relate to both the explicit and implicit aspects of the story. These are for the most part aligned with current practice and in all likelihood feel familiar.

However, anchor standard one (R.CCR.1) represents a shift in practice, as it introduces how to regularly use textual evidence to support conclusions. In kindergarten, this is mostly accomplished by requiring students to answer questions about the details in a text; in first and second grades this practice is further expanded to include who, what, where, when, why, and how questions. Citing evidence from the text can be a challenge for students who have become accustomed to stating their thoughts and opinions without referring back to the text. Building the habit of referring to the text requires a shift in instruction, especially in our questioning habits. Regularly using text-dependent questions can drive young readers back to the text and reinforce selective re-reading and look-backs as methods to support deeper comprehension (Bossert & Schwantes, 1995).

Remembering to ask text-dependent questions requires preparation. After all, it is much easier to ask more general questions about a selection, especially the kind that allows students to make personal connections. However, these don't advance student knowledge of the reading itself and can derail classroom discussions about a text. As depicted in figure 2.2, there are six types of questions that require students to use evidence from the text in their responses.

These question types represent a progression of increasingly more complex understandings, with literal-level knowledge forming the foundation from which the questions move toward inferential meaning and critical analysis.

1. **General understanding questions:** Teachers pose these questions in order to determine whether students grasp the overall meaning of the text. While they may appear more global in nature, they are crafted so that students are required to *explain* as well as *describe.* Hannah Kohl asks a general understanding question of her kindergarten students who are reading *The Very Hungry Caterpillar* (Carle, 1969), "Can you retell the text using the words, *beginning, middle,* and *end*?" Tanya says, "In the beginning, the caterpillar is a little egg on a leaf!" Alexis adds, "In the middle, he eats a lot and gets his stomachache." Marco says, "At the end, he's a butterfly. He has a lot of colors, not like when he was a caterpillar."

2. **Key detail questions:** These questions build on the foundational knowledge needed for general understanding by drawing attention to critical details that relate to the whole. When Ms. Kohl asks, "How many days did it take to go from an egg to a caterpillar?" Ramzy answers, "It took more than three weeks because he ate for one week, then it says right here on page twenty, 'He stayed inside for more than two weeks.'" Ms. Kohl then asks, "Which foods gave

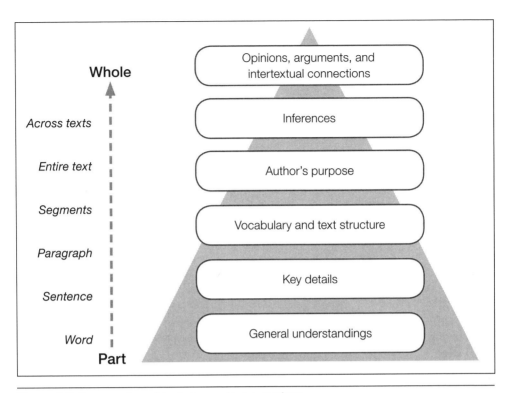

Figure 2.2: Progression of text-dependent questions.

him a stomachache and which foods did not?" The students search for the information, and Ms. Kohl charts their responses.

3. **Vocabulary and text structure questions:** These questions bridge the literal-level meanings of a text to move toward inferential interpretations. Questions regarding word choice, use of figurative language, and organization of information further build students' understanding of the author's craft. Ms. Kohl asks a question that requires students to determine the meaning of unknown words: "How does the author help us understand the word *cocoon*?" The class discusses the fact that the author uses an illustration to help. In addition, Jeremy notices a sentence on p. 20 that reads, "'He built a small house, called a cocoon, around himself.'" Tanya says, "So it's like a house, and he goes inside to sleep so he could become a butterfly."

4. **Author's purpose questions:** These questions invite students to step back from the text in order to examine the reading's effect on an audience and to look closely for clues that illuminate the author's intentions. These questions may focus on genre and narration or require students to engage in critical analysis in determining whether another viewpoint is missing. The text type itself shapes the author's purpose questions. Ms. Kohl wants her students to examine the narrator, which can help them determine if the text is narrative or informational. She asks, "Who tells us about the events: the caterpillar or a narrator?"

Her students search the text again, and Mario says, "It's a narrator, because he says *he* and *his*." She probes, "If the caterpillar were telling the story, which words would he use?" Sarah says, "He would say *I* or *me*."

5. **Inferencing questions:** These questions further the progression toward deeper understanding by requiring students to locate the nuances of a literary text, examine the arguments contained in a persuasive piece, or probe the details of major ideas in an informational text passage. One of the inference questions Ms. Kohl asks requires that students use the details from the text to analyze the title. She says, "The title of the book is *The Very Hungry Caterpillar*. How do we know he is hungry?" Jessica says, "After he ate the apple, he was still hungry." Sarah adds, "And when he ate three plums he was still hungry." Mario says, "And he ate all of those things that hurt his stomach, so he must be very hungry!"

6. **Opinions, arguments, and intertextual connection questions:** These questions advance students' thinking about the broader meanings of a text by foregrounding it against a backdrop of personal experiences and inviting comparisons across texts. When these questions are delayed until after students have had a chance to read and re-read a text, the discussions themselves are richer and more complex. Ms. Kohl asks her students, "Is this a happy story or a sad one? How do you know?" Khalid answers, "It's happy because he changed into a beautiful butterfly." Sarah counters, "I think it's kinda sad because he was hungry all the time and then he got sick." The next week, the class reads *Monarch Butterfly* (Gibbons, 1991b), and Ms. Kohl adds another question, "How is this book like *The Very Hungry Caterpillar* we read last week, and how is it different?"

Although these examples are based on reading an informational text, comparable questions are just as useful with literary text. Second-grade teacher Maria Green uses text-dependent questions with her students, many of whom are English learners.

"Our team chose *The Raft* [LaMarche, 2000] for several reasons. The readability level is second grade. We have lots of English learners, so we wanted to keep the readability manageable so we could pay closer attention to the qualitative factors in this book," she says. "There's lots of inferring students need to do to understand the story."

She joins a discussion group of students after it had read the text and she had read it to the class.

"I've got some questions of my own, and I want you to use your book as you think about them," she says. "Don't ever think that being an effective reader means you have to keep everything in your head. I want you to look back. How does the raft change Nicky's time with his grandmother?"

Marcus responds, "He's worried that there's no TV so he'll be bored." Avery says, "Yeah, but then he tries to get his chores done fast so that he can go on the raft." Ms. Green acknowledges, "Yes, that's true. Why does Grandma call the birds *hitchhikers*?"

Rochelle answers, "They follow along the raft. It says right here on page fourteen that they 'kept us company.'" Ms. Green adds, "Is that what it means, *hitchhiking*? Read some more and see what you think."

After a few moments, Rochelle says, "Oh, later it says that they landed on the raft and took a ride. So, it means that they didn't have to work, like they got to go along on the ride for free." Ms. Green exclaims, "There you go! Who gave Nicky the raft? Or who drew the other pictures of the animals?" Avery observes, "I think it was his grandma. I don't think it just came along, because she was not surprised when he had it, and she even went with him to show him how to use it." Marcus adds, "Like maybe she snuck it there so he would find it." Ms. Green says, "That's a great example of inferring. The author didn't say this outright, but you were drawing conclusions on your own. So now here's another question, Why does Nick draw a picture of a deer on the raft before he leaves? Remember to use your book." Marcus answers, "I think it is because he saved the life of the baby deer that was stuck." Avery says, "Maybe people saved all of the animals on the raft. I just thought of that. Maybe people drew them when they did something really special." Ms. Green asks, "Can you find evidence for that?"

For the next few minutes, the group discusses its ideas about the drawings, but the students cannot find evidence in the text. Avery says, "I guess that was just a feeling I had. But I can't find anything that says that. I do think that the raft made him like staying with his grandma better." Marcus adds, "I agree. And he learned about animals, like what the otters do and how to fish."

Ms. Green uses similar text-dependent questions in discussions with other groups as well. For example:

- "How do Nicky's interactions with the animals change during the story?" (general understanding)
- "What is he going to use the rope for?" (key detail)
- "What is a *river rat,* and why does he call himself one?" (vocabulary and text structure)
- "What does the author want you to learn from this story?" (author's purpose)
- "How did Nicky's grandma change his opinion about the river?" (inferencing)
- "Are his memories going to be fond ones or not?" (opinions, arguments, and intertextual connection)

Craft and Structure in Literature

The language of structure in literature dominates this domain (see table 2.5, page 40). Beginning in kindergarten, students are encouraged to recognize common text types and initially identify the differences between narrative and informational texts. The commonly taught early storybook knowledge of illustrators and authors is present in kindergarten, but by second grade this has deepened considerably, as young readers begin to analyze points of view among characters. In addition, second-grade students

Table 2.5: Literature Standards for Domain Craft and Structure, Grades K–2

Anchor Standards	Kindergarten Standards	Grade 1 Standards	Grade 2 Standards
R.CCR.4: Interpret words and phrases as they are used in a text, determining technical, connotative, and figurative meanings, and analyze how specific word choices shape meaning or tone.	**RL.K.4:** Ask and answer questions about unknown words in a text.	**RL.1.4:** Identify words or phrases in stories or poems that suggest feelings or appeal to the senses.	**RL.2.4:** Describe how words and phrases (such as regular beats, alliteration, rhymes, and repeated lines) supply rhythm and meaning in a story, poem, or song.
R.CCR.5: Analyze the structure of texts, including how specific sentences, paragraphs, and larger portions of the text (such as a section, chapter, scene, or stanza) relate to each other and the whole.	**RL.K.5:** Recognize common types of texts (such as storybooks and poems).	**RL.1.5:** Explain major differences between books that tell stories and books that give information, drawing on a wide reading of a range of text types.	**RL.2.5:** Describe the overall structure of a story, including describing how the beginning introduces the story and the ending concludes the story.
R.CCR.6: Assess how point of view or purpose shapes the content and style of a text.	**RL.K.6:** With prompting and support, name the author and illustrator of a story and define the role of each in telling the story.	**RL.1.6:** Identify who is telling the story at various points in a text.	**RL.2.6:** Acknowledge differences in the points of view of characters, including speaking in a different voice for each character when reading dialogue aloud.

Source: Adapted from NGA & CCSSO, 2010a, pp. 10 and 11.

look at how the sounds and meanings of words play an important role in poetry and song and provide alliteration in stories.

The twenty-three kindergarten students in Anya Lee's class have assembled on the rug around her rocking chair. To her left is an easel with a big-book version of *Baby Gets Dressed* (Cowley, 1989). This predictable text contains a simple two-word pattern on each page depicting a toddler being dressed after her bath. Predictable texts present a pattern that assists emergent readers in anticipating the words on the page. Ms. Lee begins by holding the book upside down and backward. As the children giggle and protest, she asks them what's wrong. Moishe calls out, "You're holding it wrong!" Ms. Lee then asks him to come up to place the book correctly on the easel. She then identifies the front cover and back cover of the book and locates the names of the author and illustrator. To activate background knowledge and support comprehension, she asks the students questions about the picture of the baby on the front cover. Several students make personal connections regarding their younger brothers and sisters, but Ms. Lee brings the discussion back to the main idea of the story: helping a young child get dressed.

In addition to book-handling skills, Ms. Lee knows that these emergent readers need practice with one-to-one matching of spoken words to print. After reading the entire book to the students to familiarize them with the pattern, she begins the story again, placing highlighter tape over each word that represents an article of clothing. She then reads the book using a wooden pointer to move carefully under each word as she reads it. She begins the story a fourth time, inviting students to come up to the easel to read and point with her. Each time, they locate and discuss the title, author, and illustrator. Ms. Lee provides physical and gestural prompts when needed to support each student's effort, deliberately choosing children whom she anticipates will need extra help. For example, when Angela struggles with pointing to the words as she reads, Ms. Lee uses hand-over-hand, a physical prompt, to guide Angela in tracking the words. When Jorge mispronounces a word, Ms. Lee points to the first letter of the word, a gestural prompt. Meanwhile, she has the rest of the students clap once as each word is read. Although subtle, the physical movement and sound each student generates serve as a cue.

Integration of Knowledge and Ideas in Literature

Only two of the three anchor standards appear in this part, as argumentation is not commonly utilized in fiction (see table 2.6, page 42). Across the grade band, anchor standard seven (R.CCR.7) in the domain expects students to examine the relationship between illustrations and text. Many of the read-aloud text exemplars listed in appendix B of the CCSS (NGA & CCSSO, 2010c) offer such opportunities. *Kitten's First Full Moon* (Henkes, 2004), a Caldecott Medal winner, is an example of such a text. Each year the Association for Library Service to Children, a division of the American Library Association, awards the Caldecott Medal to books that exemplify the "collective unity of story-line, theme, or concept" that "provides a child with a visual experience" (ALA, 2012). These books are excellent sources for developing students' ability to notice the relationship between illustration and text.

Other familiar elements in this domain include the emphasis on looking across stories to notice similarities and differences in anchor standard nine (R.CCR.9). A familiar example suitable for second grade is the Cinderella story archetype that appears in the oral and written traditions of so many cultures.

Table 2.6: Literature Standards for Domain Integration of Knowledge and Ideas, Grades K–2

Anchor Standards	Kindergarten Standards	Grade 1 Standards	Grade 2 Standards
R.CCR.7: Integrate and evaluate content presented in diverse media and formats, including visually and quantitatively, as well as in words.	**RL.K.7**: With prompting and support, describe the relationship between illustrations and the story in which they appear (for example, what moment in a story an illustration depicts).	**RL.1.7:** Use illustrations and details in a story to describe characters, setting, or events.	**RL.2.7:** Use information gained from the illustrations and words in a print or digital text to demonstrate understanding of its characters, setting, or plot.
R.CCR.8: Delineate and evaluate the argument and specific claims in a text, including the validity of the reasoning as well as the relevance and sufficiency of the evidence.	n/a	n/a	n/a
R.CCR.9: Analyze how two or more texts address similar themes or topics in order to build knowledge or to compare the approaches the authors take.	**RL.K.9:** With promoting and support, compare and contrast adventures and experiences of characters in familiar stories.	**RL.1.9:** Compare and contrast the adventures and experiences of characters in stories.	**RL.2.9:** Compare and contrast two or more versions of the same story (such as Cinderella stories) by different authors or from different cultures.

Source: Adapted from NGA & CCSSO, 2010a, pp. 10 and 11.

The focus on visual literacy in anchor standard seven (R.CCR.7) is likely to represent a genuine departure from what most elementary educators teach. While extracting information from illustrations is common for emergent readers, the dominance of text in second grade often means that this form of literacy is left behind. But note that digital text is specifically mentioned in grade 2, in preparation for the multiliteracies that become prominent in third grade. Movement, light, sound, and images comprise these elements (Frey, Fisher, & Gonzalez, 2010). Second-grade teacher Don Wilson explains the effects of e-books on his teaching, "I'm using more e-books now, and it's really challenging me and my students in understanding how these two environments are alike and different. One thing I've discovered is that there's a pretty controlled progression to the story in a print book," he said. "However, on a digital platform, it's easier for the reader to jump around, and even skip important parts. So we talk about the habits of readers, such as persistence and the self-discipline to read an entire story all the way through."

Range of Reading and Level of Text Complexity

Anchor standard ten (R.CCR.10) in this domain is brief but heavily influences much of the instruction across all the domains and other standards. Looking at the K–2 grade band, one can see how text complexity and scaffolded instruction intersect (see table 2.7). The second-grade standard (R.2.10) references the grades 2–3 text exemplars and further notes that students should be able to read similar stories and poems "proficiently, with scaffolding as needed, at the high end of the range" (NGA & CCSSO, 2010a, p. 12). The grades 2–3 band is further defined as 420–820L (see table 2.1, page 29). This range is broader than that MetaMetrics previously defined for the 2–3 grade-level band (450–725L). As noted in table 2.1 (page 29), these are revised measures for Common Core ELA (CCSSO, 2012).

Table 2.7: Literature Standards for Domain Range of Reading and Text Complexity, Grades K–2

Anchor Standard	Kindergarten Standard	Grade 1 Standard	Grade 2 Standard
	n/a	n/a	**Lexile range 420–820L* (grades 2–3 band)**
R.CCR.10: Read and comprehend complex literary and informational texts independently and proficiently.	**R.K.10:** Actively engage in group reading activities with purpose and understanding.	**R.1.10:** With prompting and support, read prose and poetry of appropriate complexity for grade 1.	**R.2.10:** By the end of the year, read and comprehend literature, including stories and poetry, in the grades 2–3 text complexity band proficiently, with scaffolding as needed at the high end of the range.

* This is a quantitative measure only and includes grade 3. Full assessment of text complexity must also include qualitative factors and reader and task considerations.

Source: Adapted from NGA & CCSSO, 2010a, pp. 10–11.

These text complexity levels are likely to be challenging for many students, but keep in mind that these are end-of-year expectations. Furthermore, merely giving students difficult texts and then expecting them to somehow read them is a sure recipe for failure (Allington, 2002). In order for students to be able to read and comprehend more difficult texts, students require purposeful instruction that relies on a gradual release of responsibility model of instruction (Frey, Fisher, & Nelson, 2010; Pearson & Gallagher, 1983).

The key to addressing text complexity in grades K–2 is to note the active role of the teacher. In kindergarten, the emphasis is on group reading activities, as students are not commonly reading independently. In first grade, prompting and support are integral to instruction. Although students are in the early reading stage of development, they are still building the cognitive stamina needed for sustained reading. Even in second grade, scaffolding continues to be important, as students further extend their growing ability to read for sustained periods of time.

Reading Standards for Informational Text in Grades K–2

The Reading Standards for Informational Text parallel the Reading Standards for Literature. These standards describe the uses of content-rich nonfiction trade books that focus on a concept or topic, biographies and autobiographies, photographic essays, procedural texts, and texts that draw from primary-source documents (Moss, 2003). Informational texts can and should be used across disciplines, and not only in the reading and language arts block, as they are equally as valuable for building content knowledge as they are as reading instruction materials. Like the literature exemplars in appendix B of the CCSS (NGA & CCSSO, 2010c), informational text exemplars are organized as a K–1 band and a separate grades 2–3 band. Table 2.8 lists sample texts.

Table 2.8: Exemplars for Informational Texts in Grades K–2

Genre	Kindergarten	Grade 1	Grade 2
Informational Texts	Hoban (1987): *I Read Signs*	Aliki (1989): *My Five Senses*	Ruffin (2000): *Martin Luther King, Jr. and the March on Washington*
Read-Aloud Informational Texts	Jenkins (2003): *What Do You Do With a Tail Like This?*	Hodgkins (2007): *How People Learned to Fly*	Wick (1997): *A Drop of Water: A Book of Science and Wonder*

Source: Adapted from NGA & CCSSO, 2010c.

As with the standards for literature, the informational text standards emanate from the same anchor standards. One noticeable difference is that anchor standard eight (R.CCR.8), which concerns argumentation, is represented in the informational text part of the Reading standards. In the same fashion that your collaborative team analyzed the standards for literature, we invite you to do the same in this section using the four-part protocol described in figure 2.1 (page 26): (1) What is familiar? (2) What is new? (3) What may be challenging for students? (4) What may be challenging for teachers? (Visit **go.solution-tree.com/commoncore** for an online-only reproducible of figure 2.1 that you can use for this analysis with your collaborative team.)

Key Ideas and Details in Informational Texts

The grade-level standards for this domain are similar to those for literature in the sense that they require students to locate key ideas and main topics of stated information with support and prompting (kindergarten), progressing in their ability to do so on their own in grade 1 and being able to do so in longer texts in grade 2 (see table 2.9). As a reminder, the use of text-based questions is especially valuable in encouraging students to engage in multiple readings. Re-reading is particularly important when students are reading conceptually dense informational texts. In addition, understanding the relationships between ideas, concepts, or events also grows across the three grades, with students examining the internal construction of the content knowledge as the author explains and discusses it.

Table 2.9: Informational Text Standards for Domain Key Ideas and Details, Grades K–2

Anchor Standards	Kindergarten Standards	Grade 1 Standards	Grade 2 Standards
R.CCR.1: Read closely to determine what the text says explicitly and to make logical inferences from it; cite specific textual evidence when writing or speaking to support conclusions drawn from the text.	**RI.K.1:** With prompting and support, ask and answer questions about key details in a text.	**RI.1.1:** Ask and answer questions about key details in a text.	**RI.2.1:** Ask and answer such questions as *who, what, where, when, why,* and *how* to demonstrate understanding of key details in a text.
R.CCR.2: Determine central ideas of themes of a text and analyze their development; summarize the key supporting details and ideas.	**RI.K.2:** With prompting and support, identify the main topic and retell key details of a text.	**RI.1.2:** Identify the main topic and retell key details of a text.	**RI.2.2:** Identify the main topic of a multiparagraph text as well as the focus of specific paragraphs within the text.
R.CCR.3: Analyze how and why individuals, events, and ideas develop and interact over the course of a text.	**RI.K.3:** With prompting and support, describe the connection between two individuals, events, ideas, or pieces of information in a text.	**RI.1.3:** Describe the connection between two individuals, events, ideas, or pieces of information in a text.	**RI.2.3:** Describe the connection between a series of historical events, scientific ideas or concepts, or steps in technical procedures in a text.

Source: Adapted from NGA & CCSSO, 2010a, pp. 10 and 13.

First-grade teacher Mikayla Washington routinely uses text-dependent questions to promote deep reading with her students. Using the book *How Animals Shed Their Skin* (Tatham, 2002) as a read-aloud, the class discusses the section on how reptiles do so. Ms. Washington asks questions that cause the students to return to the pages of the book, and she reminds them to support their answers with textual evidence. In order to make sure they have a general understanding of the passage, Ms. Washington asks them about similarities and differences among reptiles. She prompts them to pay close attention to the last paragraph, which explains that "some reptiles face dangers while shedding their skin . . . [but] others have it much easier" (Tatham, 2002, p. 41). She further prompts them about the key details contained in the text. Together, she and the students make a chart listing the dangers, including exposure to the sun (lizards), temporary blindness (snakes), and an inability to run (snakes). On another chart they list the animals—such as tortoises, alligators, and crocodiles—that don't experience these problems during shedding because "it flakes off a little at a time" (p. 41). "I really want the students to look carefully at these main ideas and details, because it's foundational knowledge for what comes next," Ms. Washington explains. "How can I expect them to infer and formulate opinions when they don't have an understanding of key ideas and details?"

Craft and Structure in Informational Texts

This domain emphasizes solving unknown words and phrases within a larger piece of text and the organizational structures and features that tie these to conceptual knowledge such as headings, glossaries, and bold print (see table 2.10). Anchor standards five (R.CCR.5) and six (R.CCR.6) deserve special attention, because together they invite students to consider how illustrations, photographs, and other text features contribute to one's overall understanding of the text.

Carlos Fernandez is working with a small group of his kindergarten students to introduce them to unfamiliar text features. They have read *Shoes, Shoes, Shoes* (Morris, 1995) several times in their guided reading group and have become familiar with the content of this text. In one lesson, Mr. Fernandez uses a *close-reading approach* to focus discussion on features of a text (Fisher et al., 2012; Richards, 1929). A guided close reading of a worthy passage consists of:

- An initial independent reading to gain familiarity with the text

- Annotations of the text to note patterns, confusions, and connections

- Think-alouds to scaffold comprehension

- Text-dependent questions

- Discussion using evidence from the text

- Opportunities to re-read the passage, both in its entirety and using selective portions of the passage

Table 2.10: Informational Text Standards for Domain Craft and Structure, Grades K–2

Anchor Standards	Kindergarten Standards	Grade 1 Standards	Grade 2 Standards
R.CCR.4: Interpret words and phrases as they are used in a text, including determining technical, connotative, and figurative meanings, and analyze how specific word choices shape meaning or tone.	**RI.K.4:** With prompting and support, ask and answer questions about unknown words in a text.	**RI.1.4:** Ask and answer questions to help determine or clarify the meaning of words or phrases in a text.	**RI.2.4:** Determine the meaning of words and phrases in a text relevant to a *grade 2 topic or subject area.*
R.CCR.5: Analyze the structure of texts, including how specific sentences, paragraphs, and larger portions of the text (such as a section, chapter, scene, or stanza) relate to each other and the whole.	**RI.K.5:** Identify the front cover, back cover, and title page of a book.	**RI.1.5:** Know and use various text features (such as headings, tables of contents, glossaries, electronic menus, and icons) to locate key facts or information in a text.	**RI.2.5:** Know and use various text features (such as captions, bold print, subheadings, glossaries, indexes, electronic menus, and icons) to locate key facts or information in a text efficiently.
R.CCR.6: Assess how point of view or purpose shapes the content and style of a text.	**RI.K.6:** Name the author and illustrator of a text and define the role of each in presenting the ideas or information in a text.	**RI.1.6:** Distinguish between information provided by pictures or other illustrations and information provided by words in a text.	**RI.2.6:** Identify the main purpose of a text, including what the author wants to answer, explain, or describe.

Source: Adapted from NGA & CCSSO, 2010a, pp. 10 and 13.

Mr. Fernandez begins by reminding students they have read this book before, and he invites them to read it again to be reminded about the content. "We're going to look at this book again, and I'm going to ask you questions. You'll use your books to find the answers." He goes on to explain that there is information in the book beyond the story. Over the course of a few minutes, he asks the five students in the group to find the information and show where they found it, using the following questions.

- Who is the author of the book?
- What page tells us about *work shoes*?
- What page tells us about *walking shoes*?

This last question proves to be more difficult, as the page number is not shown. The previous page is *page nineteen*. Together, the students figure out that *page twenty* must be the answer for the question about walking shoes. Mr. Fernandez repeats these questions several more times, giving students practice at locating page numbers on marked and unmarked pages. He then directs their attention to the index. "The author put more information about the photographs in the back of the book. I can read this information to you, but you'll need to tell me the page number where the photograph appears. Then we can look it up together." The students learn that the photograph of the ballerina's slippers on page five was taken in Russia, and they are called *toe shoes*. Olinda is delighted to learn that the photograph on page eighteen was taken in her native Colombia. Most of all, the students like learning that the shoe-shaped house on the title page is in Pennsylvania, their home state. "It will take lots more practice, don't get me wrong," Mr. Fernandez remarks later to his collaborative team. "But this activity gives them a solid introduction into using some of these text features to get more out of a familiar book."

Integration of Knowledge and Ideas in Informational Texts

This domain highlights the importance of young readers' ability to infer information within and across texts and to process visual and textual details cohesively (see table 2.11). In addition, readers are asked to notice the evidence an author uses to support an idea or concept. These are subtle points, and inexperienced readers are likely to rush past these details. Noticing details takes time. Therefore, to foster deep comprehension and to enable students to determine levels of meaning in order, teachers need to slow down the pace of instruction.

Krista Egan has conducted a series of close reading lessons with her first-grade students using the book *Oceans* (Daniels, 1999). In a shared reading lesson, Ms. Egan projects the two pages devoted to the kelp forests onto the interactive whiteboard so her students can view the text features. Before reading the text, she draws their attention to the heading, and to activate their background knowledge, she reminds them, "Put your ocean hats on!" She explains, "The author uses that subheading so I can organize my thinking. I've got to remember where kelp forests are, and what I know about them." Then she asks, "Does this heading bring any questions to mind?" After a moment, Kara hesitantly says, "How can there be a forest in an ocean?" "There you go! Now you're thinking!" Ms. Egan exclaims. "When I make a question in my head, it gives me something to watch out for. I want the author to answer this." She reads the main portion of the text to her students, as they are not yet able to read it independently. Over the next ten minutes the students identify the definition of kelp (*largest plants in the ocean* and *huge seaweeds*) as individual students highlight these phrases on the board. This activity gives them experience annotating text. They analyze the two accompanying photographs and infer from the murky waters that kelp forests are dark. After reading the two captions Ms. Egan asks, "Does the author ever tell you it's dark?" The students note that the author does not. "Then how do you know?" Ms. Egan persists. She wants the students to make

Table 2.11: Informational Text Standards for Domain Integration of Knowledge and Ideas, Grades K–2

Anchor Standards	Kindergarten Standards	Grade 1 Standards	Grade 2 Standards
R.CCR.7: Integrate and evaluate content presented in diverse media and format, including visually and quantitatively, as well as in words.	**RI.K.7:** With prompting and support, describe the relationship between illustrations and the text in which they appear (like what person, place, thing, or idea in the text an illustration depicts).	**RI.1.7:** Use the illustrations and details in a text to describe its key ideas.	**RI.2.7:** Explain how specific images (such as a diagram showing how a machine works) contribute to and clarify a text.
R.CCR.8: Delineate and evaluate the argument and specific claims in a text including the validity of the reasoning as well as the relevance and sufficiency of the evidence.	**RI.K.8:** With prompting and support, identify the reasons an author gives to support points in a text.	**RI.1.8:** Identify the reasons an author gives to support points in a text.	**RI.2.8:** Describe how reasons support specific points the author makes in a text.
R.CCR.9: Analyze how two or more texts address similar themes or topics in order to build knowledge or to compare the approaches the authors take.	**RI.K.9:** With prompting and support, identify basic similarities and differences between two texts on the same topic (such as in illustrations, descriptions, or procedures).	**RI.1.9:** Identify basic similarities and differences between two texts on the same topic (such as in illustrations, descriptions, or procedures).	**RI.2.9:** Compare and contrast the most important points presented by two texts on the same topic.

Source: Adapted from NGA & CCSSO, 2010a, pp. 10 and 13.

connections between the photographs and the text. Michael is the first to realize, "The author didn't just pick pretty pictures to decorate the pages. She wants us to know stuff about kelp!" The class constructs a chart that illuminates the role of text and images in their learning. (See figure 2.3, page 50.)

Range of Reading and Level of Text Complexity in Informational Texts

With the exception of naming genres, the wording for anchor standard ten (R.CCR.10) in this domain is the same for informational texts as it is for literature. As illustrated in previous examples (see table 2.2, pages 31–33), determining a text's complexity and then using it with other texts in such a way—using the staircase approach—so ideas build on one another is more complex.

"The Kelp Forest" on pages 20–21 from *Oceans* by Patricia Daniels		
What We Know From the Text	**What We Know From the Photos**	**What the Text and the Photos Together Tell Us**
Kelp plants are the largest plants in the ocean. They grow a foot in a day! There is gas in the kelp leaves so they can float.	It is very dark in the kelp forest! Some of the sunlight shines down into the water, so it's lighter near the top. Maybe the creatures that live there have big eyes to see in the dark, like the seal in the picture does.	Lots of creatures live in the kelp forest. It's cold, so creatures need lots of protection to stay warm. Kelp is used in a lot of things, like ice cream, tires, and glue.

Source: Daniels, 1999.

Figure 2.3: First-grade students' analysis of photographs and text.

Teams must consider quantitative measures, qualitative factors, reader understanding, and task demand for informational texts. Qualitative measures are used exclusively in kindergarten and first grade, as the texts used for emergent and early readers cannot be reliably measured using quantitative tools. Table 2.12 shows the informational text standards for the domain range of reading and text complexity.

Table 2.12: Informational Text Standards for Domain Range of Reading and Text Complexity, Grades K–2

Anchor Standard	Kindergarten Standard	Grade 1 Standard	Grade 2 Standard
R.CCR.10: Read and comprehend complex literary and informational texts independently and proficiently.	**RI.K.10:** Actively engage in group reading activities with purpose and understanding.	**RI.1.10:** With prompting and support, read informational texts appropriately complex for grade 1.	**RI.2.10:** By the end of the year, read and comprehend informational texts, including history and social studies, science, and technical texts, in the grades 2–3 text complexity band proficiently, with scaffolding as needed at the high end of the range.

Source: Adapted from NGA & CCSSO, 2010a, pp. 10 and 13.

Your collaborative team can begin to establish a sequence of texts across grades K–2 by beginning with the texts already in use. Figure 2.4 (pages 51–52) is a protocol for teams to use as you make these determinations about text complexity. A good starting place to begin the conversation about text complexity is to refer to the text exemplars for grade 2 in appendix B of the CCSS ELA (NGA & CCSSO, 2010c). Ideally, some of the texts

Title of text: _____

Author: _____   **Publication date:** _____

Current Experiences

What is the current use of the text? (Include grade level, content area, and unit or topic.)

What have our experiences been with using this text?

What are its positive outcomes?

What are its drawbacks?

Quantitative Factors

What is the quantitative measure of this text? What measure did we use? (This applies to grade 2 only.)

Qualitative Measures

1 = Comfortable (texts that are comfortable or build background, fluency, and skills)

2 = Grade level (texts that require grade-appropriate skills)

3 = Stretch (texts that stretch a reader's thinking or require instruction)

Levels of Meaning and Purpose	Rating
Density and complexity	
Figurative language	
Purpose	
Score	

Structure	Rating
Genre	
Organization	
Narration	
Text features and graphics	
Score	

Language and Conventionality	Rating
Standard English and variations	
Register	
Score	

Knowledge Demands	Rating
Background knowledge	
Prior knowledge	
Cultural knowledge	
Vocabulary knowledge	
Score	
Total qualitative score	

continued →

Figure 2.4: Collaborative team protocol for determining text complexity.

Questions for Considering the Reader and the Task

Will this text maintain our students' attention?

Will this text require specialized supports (such as language support or accommodations)?

Does the text's topic or genre interest our students?

Does the reader possess the needed metacognitive skills to comprehend the text?

Does the reader have sufficient background or prior knowledge to link to new information?

What direct experiences do our students have that may make this text more accessible?

Does this text require modeling of comprehension and word-solving strategies?

Does the task match the readers' collaborative learning and social skills?

Does the task provide sufficient challenge for our students, while avoiding protracted frustration?

Recommendations for Using This Text

For which grade is this text most appropriate, given the qualitative and quantitative analyses?

What are the specific teaching points necessary for student understanding?

Would this text be best for whole-class instruction, small-group learning, collaborative activities, or independent tasks?

Visit **go.solution-tree.com/commoncore** for a reproducible version of this figure.

you currently use will appear on this list and can serve as placeholders for the texts team members have identified for further analysis. We suggest that the team discuss two or three texts at each meeting as a way to attune members to these considerations. As the team collectively becomes more adept at analyzing texts, pairs of teachers can collaborate to assess books for text complexity. Over time, the collaborative team can use these assessments to create a sequence of texts to be used at the beginning, middle, and end of each grade level in order to ensure that texts are being used as a staircase from one year to the next.

Foundational Skills in Reading in Grades K–2

The CCSS for reading in grades K–5 include a part, Foundational Skills, not featured in grades 6–12. As described in the Common Core ELA, these are not outcome standards, but rather necessary prerequisite skills for emergent, early, and intermediate readers (NGA & CCSSO, 2010a). Therefore, they are not tied to the anchor standards like the grade-level expectations for Literature and Informational Text. Instead, these foundational skills are organized around what Scott G. Paris (2005) calls *constrained skills*. Certain early reading skills are fundamental to breaking the code of written language (Gentry, 2006). Readers must know the sounds of the language, alphabet of the language, and the ways in which sounds are associated with letters (National Institute of Child Health and Human Development, 2000). In reading terminology, we call these concepts *phonemic awareness*, *alphabetic knowledge*, and *phonological knowledge*. Some of these skills are finite, and therefore limited (or highly constrained): the English language has forty-four phonemes and twenty-six letters in its alphabet. Fluency is also constrained, since at some point rate, pitch, intonation, and prosody converge to an end point at which reading can't go any faster. On the other hand, unconstrained skills have no end point and learning continues throughout a reader's lifetime. Vocabulary knowledge and comprehension are unconstrained. Think about it. Don't you know more vocabulary today than you did five years ago? Can't you comprehend text more ably now than when you were in college?

The K–5 Foundational Skills acknowledge the importance of, as well as the end point for, two constrained skills: (1) print concepts (like alphabetic knowledge, directionality, and spaces between words) and (2) phonological awareness, which are exclusively K–1 standards. Across grades K–5 there are two other less-constrained skills: (1) phonics and word recognition and (2) fluency. These four domains fully comprise the foundational skills in reading for grades K–2.

Print Concepts

Print concepts are exclusively defined at kindergarten and first-grade levels (see table 2.13, page 54). At kindergarten, these include directionality, the relationship between speech and print, the conceptual understanding that space between words carries meaning, and lowercase and uppercase recognition. By first grade, these are further extended to include capitalization and punctuation.

Table 2.13: Reading Standards for Foundational Skills in Print Concepts, Grades K–2

Kindergarten Standards	Grade 1 Standards	Grade 2 Standards
RF.K.1: Demonstrate understanding of the organization and basic features of print. a. Follow words from left to right, top to bottom, and page by page. b. Recognize that spoken words are represented in written language by specific sequences of letters. c. Understand that words are separated by spaces in print. d. Recognize and name all upper- and lowercase letters of the alphabet.	**RF.1.1:** Demonstrate understanding of the organization and basic features of print. a. Recognize the distinguishing features of a sentence (such as first-word capitalization and ending punctuation).	n/a

Source: Adapted from NGA & CCSSO, 2010a, p. 15.

Phonological Awareness

As with print concepts, students in kindergarten and first grade are mastering these important concepts about the sounds of the language (see table 2.14). In kindergarten, students are expected to produce rhyming words and segment and blend phonemes. As they progress in kindergarten, students learn to substitute sounds at the initial, medial, and final sounds of *consonant-vowel-consonant* (CVC) words. In first grade, students become more adept as they can now distinguish between short- and long-vowel sounds and can isolate more difficult phonemes, such as *r*-controlled vowels.

Phonics and Word Recognition

As noted, kindergarten and first-grade students are expected to demonstrate increasing awareness and competence with print concepts and phonological awareness. Although brief, these reading standards for foundational skills have implications for writing, spelling, and learning vocabulary. Phonological recognition describes the sounds of the language, whereas phonics describes the way in which sound bolts on to letters and letter combinations. This understanding is a major conceptual leap for young readers, who must be carefully taught how to make the associations between sounds and letters (see table 2.15, page 56). This understanding all comes down to our brains, which are hardwired for spoken but not written language (Frey & Fisher, 2010a). K–2 teachers should concentrate on teaching young students how to rewire their brains in order to read. In kindergarten, students are learning sound-letter relationships and developing a bank of high-frequency sight words. In addition, they are learning the phonological skill of substitution—replacing

Table 2.14: Reading Standards for Foundational Skills in Phonological Awareness, Grades K–2

Kindergarten Standards	Grade 1 Standards	Grade 2 Standards
RF.K.2: Demonstrate understanding of spoken words, syllables, and sounds (phonemes).	**RF.1.2:** Demonstrate understanding of spoken words, syllables, and sounds (phonemes).	n/a
a. Recognize and produce rhyming words.	a. Distinguish long from short vowel sounds in spoken single-syllable words.	
b. Count, pronounce, blend, and segment syllables in spoken words.	b. Orally produce single-syllable words by blending sounds (phonemes), including consonant blends.	
c. Blend and segment onsets and rimes of single-syllable spoken words.	c. Isolate and pronounce initial, medial vowel, and final sounds (phonemes) in spoken single-syllable words.	
d. Isolate and pronounce the initial, medial vowel, and final sounds (phonemes) in three-phoneme (*consonant-vowel-consonant*, or *CVC*) words. (This does not include CVCs ending with /l/, /r/, or /x/.)	d. Segment spoken single-syllable words into their complete sequence of individual sounds (phonemes).	
e. Add or substitute individual sounds (phonemes) in simple, one-syllable words to make new words.		

Source: Adapted from NGA & CCSSO, 2010a, p. 15.

a single letter to transform a word (for example, *cat* to *mat*). In first grade, spelling-sound correspondence is extended to blends and digraphs, and students can read and write two-syllable words, including those with inflectional endings. In second grade, students are applying these skills to decode words with affixes and irregularly spelled words.

Aurelia Halvorsen frequently uses poems and song lyrics to teach her first-grade students about word families. Word families (also called *rimes*) are groups of rhyming words that end with the same vowels and consonants. For example, *thing*, *bring*, and *spring* are all part of the *-ing* word family. In addition, her students are learning to use a variety of onsets to decode words and create new ones. The onset consists of the first consonant letters up to the first vowel. In the word *spring*, *spr-* is the onset and *-ing* is the rime. Ms. Halvorsen has selected a poem featuring the *-ing* word family to use as the basis of a focus lesson on sound and symbol correspondence.

Table 2.15: Reading Standards for Foundational Skills in Phonics and Word Recognition, Grades K–2

Kindergarten Standards	Grade 1 Standards	Grade 2 Standards
RF.K.3: Know and apply grade-level phonics and word analysis skills in decoding words. a. Demonstrate basic knowledge of one-to-one letter-sound correspondences by producing the primary or many of the most frequent sounds for each consonant. b. Associate the long and short sounds with common spellings (graphemes) for the five major vowels. c. Read common high-frequency words by sight (like *the, of, to, you, she, my, is, are, do,* and *does*). d. Distinguish between similarly spelled words by identifying the sounds of the letters that differ.	**RF.1.3:** Know and apply grade-level phonics and word analysis skills in decoding words. a. Know the spelling-sound correspondences for common consonant digraphs. b. Decode regularly spelled one-syllable words. c. Know final -*e* and common vowel team conventions for representing long vowel sounds. d. Use knowledge that every syllable must have a vowel sound to determine the number of syllables in a printed word. e. Decode two-syllable words following basic patterns by breaking the words into syllables. f. Read words with inflectional endings. g. Recognize and read grade-appropriate irregularly spelled words.	**RF.2.3:** Know and apply grade-level phonics and word analysis skills in decoding words. a. Distinguish long and short vowels when reading regularly spelled one-syllable words. b. Know spelling-sound correspondences for additional common vowel teams. c. Decode regularly spelled two-syllable words with long vowels. d. Decode words with common prefixes and suffixes. e. Identify words with inconsistent but common spelling-sound correspondences. f. Recognize and read grade-appropriate irregularly spelled words.

Source: Adapted from NGA & CCSSO, 2010a, p. 16.

Ms. Halvorsen uses a rhyme she created called "Groundhog" on a language chart to teach her students about the /ing/ word family. The text on her chart reads:

> *Silly little thing,*
>
> *Does your shadow bring*
>
> *Something that tells me*
>
> *When we will have spring?*

Ms. Halvorsen selects this rime because her previous assessments demonstrate that the emergent readers in her class are beginning to attend to the final letters in words. She previously read aloud *It's Groundhog Day!* (Kroll, 1995) and *Gregory's Shadow* (Freeman, 2002). In science the students had previously created shadows on surfaces and viewed photographs of shadows to make predictions about what objects were used to create each one.

In this lesson, Ms. Halvorsen first reads the poem aloud to students while using a pointer under each word so they can track the sentences. She then reads it again and invites students to join in. After the second reading, the students discuss the meaning of the poem and answer the question in it. To prepare students for the third reading, Ms. Halvorsen says, "I hear words that rhyme in this poem. The rhyming words sound like /ing/. I'm going to read it again so listen closely for the words I say that sound like /ing/." This time she reads the poem slowly and pauses to emphasize the rhyming words *thing*, *bring*, *something*, and *spring*.

She then asks students to place pieces of colored transparent highlighting tape over the *-ing* portion of the rhyming words to further draw their attention to this letter combination. When Jamie needs help finding the correct letter combination in *something*, she asks him to say the word aloud to hear the sounds. This prompt helps Jamie correctly highlight the letters. After discussing the spelling and sounds of the rime, Ms. Halvorsen asks the students to think of other words that have the same ending sound. She uses alphabet letter cards to prompt their understanding. For example, when she pairs a large card with the letter /s/ on it with another bearing the letters /ing/, her students are able to quickly respond, "Sing!" Finally, she instructs her students to turn to their partner and tell one another words from the poem that are in the *-ing* word family and then write them in their word family journal. She moves around to listen to their partner talk, making anecdotal notes about individual students for assessment purposes. After this lesson is over, students use smaller versions of the same letter cards to construct new words from the *-ing* word family. Students then add them to the list begun in the word family journal.

Fluency

The ability to activate word-solving skills is necessary for fluency as well (see table 2.16, page 58). This single foundational standard is further described in terms of accuracy, rate, and prosody (the ability to read expressively). Taken together, these serve as a useful proxy for determining a young reader's comprehension (Rasinski, 2011). Fluency is assessed through oral and silent reading rates, but prosody can only be assessed though oral reading. These assessments are also measured with the use of on-level reading materials, and by first grade the student should be self-correcting errors.

Table 2.16: Reading Standards for Foundational Skills in Fluency, Grades K–2

Kindergarten Standards	Grade 1 Standards	Grade 2 Standards
RF.K.4: Read emergent-reader texts with purpose and understanding.	**RF.1.4:** Read with sufficient accuracy and fluency to support comprehension. a. Read on-level text with purpose and understanding. b. Read on-level text orally with accuracy, appropriate rate, and expression on successive readings. c. Use context to confirm or self-correct word recognition and understanding, rereading as necessary.	**RF.2.4:** Read with sufficient accuracy and fluency to support comprehension. a. Read on-level text with purpose and understanding. b. Read on-level text orally with accuracy, appropriate rate, and expression on successive readings. c. Use context to confirm or self-correct word recognition and understanding, rereading as necessary.

Source: Adapted from NGA & CCSSO, 2010a, p. 16.

In Ms. Halvorson's class, as students read and re-read the poem, they build fluency. There are several instructional approaches teachers can use to build and assess fluency in grades K–2 students, including the following.

- **Readers' theater:** Students perform from a script that they have practiced collaboratively (Martinez, Roser, & Strecker, 1999).

- **Neurological impress method:** The teacher reads aloud the same piece of text with an individual student at a slightly faster rate than the student reads independently (Flood, Lapp, & Fisher, 2005).

- **Repeated readings:** Students re-read the same piece of text several times, often with different purposes, leading to improvement in reading fluency, word recognition, and oral reading expression (Samuels, 2002).

Conclusion

The Common Core State Standards for reading build on content teachers already know. Students in grades K–2 need explicit instruction in the foundational skills of reading, as well as how to read narrative and expository texts. But the CCSS require that teachers raise their expectations and provide students with access to complex texts and scaffolded instruction to justify their ideas and opinions. To ensure that students are prepared to meet these increased expectations, teachers have to plan new lessons that allow students to consolidate their understanding and apply what they have learned. This is a tall order for an individual teacher. But when teachers work in collaborative teams within a PLC to plan instruction and review student performance, it is possible and even enjoyable. As we have noted throughout this chapter, collaborative planning teams should focus their conversations around four questions.

1. What is familiar in the CCSS at each grade level?

2. What appears to be new based on prior standards?

3. What may be challenging for students?

4. What may be challenging for teachers?

In addition, teams should engage in lesson planning and a systematic review of student performance to determine which lessons are effective for which students, and what they need to do to ensure that all students reach the standard. We will focus on common formative assessment and responding to students who do not meet the expectations during initial instruction in the final chapter of this book. Before doing so, we will explore the Common Core standards for the Writing, Speaking and Listening, and Language strands.

CHAPTER 3

Implementing the Common Core State Standards for Writing

KEY QUESTIONS

- To what extent does your team understand the Writing standards: What is the essence of this standard? What teacher actions facilitate this standard in practice? What evidence that students are learning this standard will we accept?

- How do the three major text types influence the writing assignments students complete and the genres students must learn?

- How is technology used to allow students to produce and publish their writing such that they can interact and collaborate with others?

The twenty students in Janet Thayer's first-grade class are eager to begin the lesson on this crisp October day. An oversized version of the book *Meanies* (Cowley, 1998) is on an easel, and the children are comfortably seated on a large rug. Another easel holds a large chart paper tablet and an assortment of markers. Ms. Thayer has used this book all week for a number of close readings. Today her students will be rewriting the text using the patterns of language Cowley uses in the book. Using interactive writing instruction, Ms. Thayer and her students begin to write a new story called "The Kind Ones." *Interactive writing* is a form of shared writing in which the students take turns writing the message on chart paper. After discussing how *kind ones* might behave, the students agree on the composition for the first page of their new class book.

> *What do kind ones do?*
> *They hold the door for others,*
> *They hold the door for others,*
> *They hold the door for others,*
> *That's what kind ones do.*

Ms. Thayer invites individual students to come up to the chart to add words while rehearsing the message, figuring out the encoding strategies needed to correctly spell the words, and checking the original text to ensure they are maintaining its language patterns. At the end of this lesson the students will write their own pages for inclusion in the class book. Six-year-old Julian remarks, "I love writing books! Do you think Joy Cowley gets help like this, too?"

A Collaborative Planning Team in Action

The genesis for Ms. Thayer's unit came from collaborative planning conversations with her fellow K–2 teachers. After their analysis of the Common Core State Standards for writing, the teachers identified several goals for improvement in their writing instruction. They wanted to provide students with writing models so they used a number of complex texts as mentors. In addition, they wanted students to take different perspectives in their writing and learn to write persuasively. Ms. Thayer notes, "We realized that most of the writing our students did was about their personal experiences. We wanted them to learn to analyze effective writers of narrative and expository texts and apprentice into that type of writing."

Noting that the Common Core State Standards for writing featured informational and explanatory texts, these teachers also focused on informational writing throughout the grades. "By the time students get to third grade, we want them to be familiar with how you organize your thoughts and how you support your opinion," Ms. Thayer stated.

In chapter 2, we introduced four questions for the collaborative planning team to use when analyzing and discussing the Reading standards: What is familiar in the CCSS at each grade level? What appears to be new based on prior standards? What may be challenging for students? What may be challenging for teachers? Teams may decide to continue using those questions as they investigate the writing standards. However, we propose a different tool for analysis for these standards, one that can facilitate discussion about the links between (1) standards, (2) instruction, and (3) formative assessment. Ms. Thayer's collaborative team uses a similar method when first unpacking the writing standards.

1. **Standards:** What is the essence of this standard?

2. **Instruction:** What teacher actions facilitate this standard in practice?

3. **Formative assessment:** What evidence that students are learning this standard will we accept?

Figure 3.1 shows a protocol for conducting this inquiry. (Visit **go.solution-tree.com /commoncore** for an online-only reproducible of this figure you can use with your collaborative team to analyze other writing standards.)

Anchor Standards for Writing

The college and career readiness anchor standards for writing are designed to articulate the need for a strong foundation across disciplines, audiences, and purposes. Writing, like speaking, is a form of communication. However, two important differences exist with writing: the audience is often unseen, and the product is often permanent. The fact is that we judge others by what and how they write. Too many misspellings and we wonder whether the person is careless. We assume disorganized discourse is the product of a jumbled mind. We often dismiss opinions altogether if there is nothing to back up the claims. In each case, the writer may be careful, organized, and articulate, but writing

Writing anchor standard seven (W.CCR.7): Conduct short as well as more sustained research projects based on focused questions, demonstrating understanding of the subject under investigation.

CCSS grade band: K–2

CCSS strand: Writing

Anchor standard domain: Research to Build and Present Knowledge

Grade-Level Standard	Standard: What Is the Essence of This Standard?	Instruction: What Teacher Actions Facilitate This Standard in Practice?	Formative Assessment: What Evidence That Students Are Learning This Standard Will We Accept?
Kindergarten **W.K.7:** Participate in shared research and writing projects (such as explore a number of books by a favorite author and express opinions about them).			
Grade 1 **W.1.7:** Participate in shared research and writing projects (such as explore a number of how-to books on a given topic and use them to write a sequence of instructions).			
Grade 2 **W.2.7:** Participate in shared research and writing projects (such as read a number of books on a single topic to produce a report; record science observations).			

Source: Adapted from NGA & CCSSO, 2010a, pp. 18–19.

Figure 3.1: Guiding questions for grade-by-grade analysis of the Writing standards.

Visit **go.solution-tree.com/commoncore** for a reproducible version of this figure.

may fail him or her. The anchor standards are an effort to ensure that students are able to communicate effectively in written form in order to represent themselves in the classroom, workplace, and world. There are ten anchor standards for writing, extending from kindergarten through twelfth grade. These standards are further organized into four domains: (1) Text Types and Purposes, (2) Production and Distribution of Writing, (3) Research to Build and Present Knowledge, and (4) Range of Writing (see NGA & CCSSO, 2010a, p. 8).

Text Types and Purposes

This domain has three anchor standards (W.CCR.1, 2, and 3), which define three major types of writing that are tied to their purposes—writing for argumentation, writing to inform or explain, and writing to convey real or imagined experiences. These basic text types are expressed through many writing genres, which in themselves are often a blend of two or more text types. For example, an opinion piece may include elements of argument, as well as narrative to describe the writer's perspective. Therefore, these text types should not be viewed too narrowly as a mandate to teach only three writing genres. Rather, it is an important reminder that we need to clearly link purposes for writing, not just the format for a genre. The anchor standards for this domain are:

1. Write arguments to support claims in an analysis of substantive topics or texts, using valid reasoning and relevant and sufficient evidence. (W.CCR.1)

2. Write informative/explanatory texts to examine and convey complex ideas and information clearly and accurately through the effective selection, organization, and analysis of content. (W.CCR.2)

3. Write narratives to develop real or imagined experiences or events using effective technique, well-chosen details, and well-structured event sequences. (W.CCR.3) (NGA & CCSSO, 2010a, p. 18)

Production and Distribution of Writing

This domain focuses on the communicative nature of writing. Anchor standard four (W.CCR.4) encourages us to link task, purpose, and audience to the selected genre or format. Anchor standard six (W.CCR.6) reveals how writing is lifted from a solitary and isolated act to one that involves peers, fellow writers, and teachers as well as experts across the classroom, community, and world. Anchor standard five (W.CCR.5) bridges the other two standards by articulating the processes a writer must necessarily engage with in order to communicate effectively. The anchor standards for this domain are:

4. Produce clear and coherent writing in which the development, organization, and style are appropriate to task, purpose, and audience. (W.CCR.4)

5. Develop and strengthen writing as needed by planning, revising, editing, rewriting, or trying a new approach. (W.CCR.5)

6. Use technology, including the Internet, to produce and publish writing and to interact and collaborate with others. (W.CCR.6) (NGA & CCSSO, 2010a, p. 18)

Research to Build and Present Knowledge

This domain foregrounds the importance of academic writing in anchor standards seven, eight, and nine (W.CCR.7, 8, and 9). Learners are encouraged to gather information from a variety of sources in order to investigate topics of worth. These activities should be a natural extension of the learning students engage in across their academic career—not just as consumers of information, but also as users and producers of the same. This requires that they critically analyze information sources, both literary and informational, and use this analysis in their writing to conduct inquiry and research.

7. Conduct short as well as more sustained research projects based on focused questions, demonstrating understanding of the subject under investigation. (W.CCR.7)

8. Gather relevant information from multiple print and digital sources, assess the credibility and accuracy of each source, and integrate the information while avoiding plagiarism. (W.CCR.8)

9. Draw evidence from literary or informational texts to support analysis, reflection, and research. (W.CCR.9) (NGA & CCSSO, 2010a, p. 18)

Range of Writing

Routinely is the key word in anchor standard ten (W.CCR.10). Writing is not something that is done only occasionally, but daily, and for extended periods of time in order to increase volume. As with reading, the intent is to build skill and stamina through frequent application and practice. Range of writing does not appear in grades K–2 standards, as young writers are still developing the tools and skills they need to engage in extended writing. However, by third grade, students are expected to be able to write longer pieces and spend longer periods of time writing.

10. Write routinely over extended time frames (time for research, reflection, and revision) and shorter time frames (a single sitting or a day or two) for a range of tasks, purposes, and audiences. (W.CCR.10) (NGA & CCSSO, 2010a, p. 18)

The anchor standards frame a vision for writing across grades K–12. But before analyzing the standards for grades K–2 in more detail, it is useful to gain a perspective on the development of writers from the primary grades to graduation. In understanding the behaviors of young writers, we can better interpret how these anchor standards link to grade-level expectations.

Characteristics of Writers

Classrooms are filled with students with different strengths and needs. In terms of writing, students in a given classroom do not all write equally well and do not all share the same instructional needs. As we have noted, however, the Common Core State Standards provide teachers with information about appropriate grade-level expectations for writing acumen. These standards reflect an understanding about writing development and growth through four stages: (1) emergent, (2) early, (3) transitional, and (4) self-extending. Although there is a correlation between a student's age and his or her stage of writing development, it is important to recognize the writing behaviors evident at each stage of development since classrooms are diverse places filled with students who have gaps in their experiences as well as extensive background knowledge. Table 3.1 describes the characteristics for each stage of writing.

Table 3.1: Characteristics of Writers

Emergent Writers . . .	Early Writers . . .
• Are learning how print works • See the permanence of writing • Retell events in sequence • Use simple sentence construction • Use known words prominently	• Have rapid recall of letters and known words • Will use formulaic writing • Have writing constrained by limited known words • Use story grammar • Write longer texts, although ideas may not be consistent
Transitional Writers . . .	**Self-Extending Writers . . .**
• Apply text structures in their original writing • Recognize audience • Write longer texts with sustained ideas • Use more complex sentences • Use transition phrases and conjunctions	• Communicate a purposeful direction to the audience • See writing as an extension of the writer • Write in multiple genres • Use words that are sophisticated and flexible • Engage in all aspects of editing

Visit **go.solution-tree.com/commoncore** for a reproducible version of this table.

Emergent Writers

These writers are just beginning to gain control of print and how it works. They are still learning that print carries a message and that they can create a new idea and then represent it on paper for others to appreciate. Emergent writers can generate text that retells a sequence of events in a story or in their personal lives, although the language used is likely to be fairly simple, with few complex sentences containing more than one or two ideas. Their writing contains letters and words they know, and their name is likely to be prominently featured in their texts. Emergent writers:

- Learn how print works, including spaces and punctuation
- Develop an understanding that their ideas can be written and re-read
- Integrate their ideas with known words

Early Writers

Early writers are able to more rapidly recall letters and therefore can scribe their message more quickly. However, they are prone to formulaic writing that incorporates the limited number of words they can spell. (Any first-grade teacher can testify to the plethora of student-generated sentences that begin with "I like"). These early writers are engaging in editing, as evidenced by the increase in eraser marks and crossed-out words. They can generate their own ideas for writing topics and are applying some elements of story grammar such as character, setting, plot, and problem and solution to their own writing. Later in this phase, students will begin writing multiparagraph texts, although the ideas forwarded at the beginning of the piece may get lost along the way. Early writers:

- Increase their writing speed and accuracy

- Produce longer pieces of text, although they often lose the thread of their ideas

- Generate their own stories with increasingly complex plots and characters

Transitional Writers

Students in this phase of development are actively incorporating varied approaches in their original writing. For example, they create titles for their pieces, use *grabber* sentences to gain the reader's attention, and use descriptive vocabulary to evoke a response from the reader. Indeed, recognizing the role of the audience is a hallmark of the writers in this phase of development. They are beginning to apply rudimentary structures to longer texts, such as listing directions for completing a task or writing a biography that contains the type of information expected in this literary form. Because their vocabulary has grown along with their sophistication of the language, there are more complex sentences containing multiple idea units. Students at this stage can utilize transition phrases and conjunctions to build these longer sentences. Their stamina has increased as well. Both mean sentence length and overall length of the text have increased. An important indicator of a transitional writer is his or her ability to sustain an idea or concept over the course of multiple paragraphs.

Students in the transitional phase of writing are engaged in using a wide range of genres in their writing. They can write short informational reports using academic vocabulary, create multiparagraph essays on personal experiences, and construct original poems. Their writing uses more regular spelling and grammatical structures but often confuses irregular forms of words or grammar (for example, *mouses* instead of *mice; have went* instead of *have gone*). They use compound sentences.

Although this phase, like the others, is not strictly bound by grade level, many transitional writers emerge between grades 3–5. While some advanced second-grade writers may already be in this phase, it is essential to know where all your writers are headed. These transitional writers are more cognizant of the processes associated with writing and are revising more of their work based on feedback from peers and the teacher, although this is more likely to be at the sentence and paragraph level rather than the document level. They are becoming more sophisticated in their use of multiple sources of information to support their own writing. Transitional writers:

- Write in multiple genres (for example, poetry, informational reports, narratives, and persuasive essays)

- Engage in author studies to examine the craft of writing (for example, an author study of Daniel Handler to learn irony or Christopher Paul Curtis to learn dialogue)

- Write rules and procedures for a variety of activities to practice technical writing (for example, directions for travel to and from school to the student's home)

- Create persuasive pieces to support a position (for example, "Why I should have a pet")

Self-Extending Writers

These sophisticated writers understand they are engaged in a complex process that is influenced by their application of specific strategies. This metacognitive awareness serves them well in being able to analyze their own writing as well as the writing of others. Self-extending writers are expanding their repertoire of writing genres and can write narratives, persuasive essays, technical documents, responses to literature, and biographies and autobiographies. Importantly, they understand that each of these genres has specific rules; the skills used to create a science lab report differ from writing a poem. Their control of the language, especially as it applies to vocabulary and multiple meanings, makes it easier for them to engage in a full editing process.

Students in this writing phase are notable for their ability to select the appropriate genre to match the task. They are learning to organize their ideas for longer pieces so that the plot moves well (for narrative) or the information is described in a logical manner (for expository). They increasingly use more complex sentences, and their word choice becomes more precise. Self-extending writers work toward two ideals: concise and precise. Their ability to edit is more sophisticated, and they are more likely to re-read their writing and retool sentences or sections to more clearly support subsequent text. Self-extending writers:

- Operate flexibly between genres (that is, they can develop multiple forms of writing during the same day)

- Seek peer and teacher feedback and integrate it into their writing

- Recognize the value of using a wide variety of sources to develop their writing and seek original sources, not just those the teacher provides

- Use accurate and innovative punctuation, word choice, and grammatical structures

- Demonstrate individual voice and style

- Utilize writing as a means of clarifying their own thinking

Samples of Student Writing

Observing how students are developing as writers is an important aspect of teaching writing well. The Common Core ELA contain a collection of student writing examples that will enable you and your collaborative team to gain added insights into what student writing looks like at various stages. As a future task for your team, use the annotated student writing examples for grades K–2 featured in appendix C of the CCSS (NGA & CCSSO, 2010d). Collectively, these samples reflect a range of writing ability and were constructed under several conditions, including on-demand writing, as well as more polished pieces that were developed through several rounds of editing and revision. These include narrative and informative and explanatory pieces at all three grade levels, as well as opinion pieces from writers in kindergarten and second grade. We encourage your team to examine these samples together across the grade-level band in order to gain a better sense of the progression to look for with emergent and early writers. These samples can serve as anchor papers for developing a consensus scoring procedure to be used at each grade level. These consensus scoring events serve as a tuning process for educators and provide valuable formative assessment data for making instructional decisions.

As we have noted previously, the Common Core State Standards articulate expectations for students across grade levels based on a common set of anchor standards. We'll explore the specific writing standards for grades K–2 in the following section.

Writing Standards for Grades K–2

The grade-level standards for writing are organized in the same manner as the domains they are derived from: Text Types and Purposes, Production and Distribution of Writing, Research to Build and Present Knowledge, and Range of Writing (NGA & CCSSO, 2010a). We hope that teachers will meet in their collaborative planning teams to discuss these standards using the protocol introduced at the beginning of this chapter.

1. **Standards:** What is the essence of this standard?

2. **Instruction:** What teacher actions facilitate this standard in practice?

3. **Formative assessment:** How will we know when each student has acquired the essential knowledge and skills?

Text Types and Purposes

The first three standards in this domain define three basic text types used in and out of school: (1) opinion, (2) informative and explanatory, and (3) narrative (see table 3.2, page 70). Although the anchor standard calls the first *argument*, the NGA and CCSSO (2010b) acknowledge that young writers are not yet developmentally situated to write for formal arguments:

> They develop a variety of methods to extend and elaborate their work by providing examples, offering reasons for their assertions, and explaining cause and effect. These kinds of expository structures are steps on the road to argument. (p. 23)

Table 3.2: Writing Standards for Domain Text Types and Purposes, Grades K–2

Anchor Standards	Kindergarten Standards	Grade 1 Standards	Grade 2 Standards
W.CCR.1: Write arguments to support claims in an analysis of substantive topics, using valid reasoning and relevant and sufficient evidence.	**W.K.1:** Use a combination of drawing, dictating, and writing to compose opinion pieces in which they tell a reader the topic or the name of the book they are writing about and state an opinion or preference about the topic or book (such as "My favorite book is . . .").	**W.1.1:** Write opinion pieces in which they introduce the topic or name of the book they are writing about, state an opinion, supply a reason for the opinion, and provide some sense of closure.	**W.2.1:** Write opinion pieces in which they introduce the topic or book they are writing about, state an opinion, supply reasons that support the opinion, use linking words (such as *because*, *and*, and *also*) to connect opinion and reasons, and provide a concluding statement or section.
W.CCR.2: Write informative and explanatory texts to examine and convey complex ideas and information clearly and accurately through the effective selection, organization, and analysis of content.	**W.K.2:** Use a combination of drawing, dictating, and writing to compose informative and explanatory texts in which they name what they are writing about and supply some information about the topic.	**W.1.2:** Write informative and explanatory texts in which they name a topic, supply some facts about the topic, and provide some sense of closure.	**W.2.2:** Write informative and explanatory texts in which they introduce a topic, use facts and definitions to develop points, and provide a concluding statement or section.
W.CCR.3: Write narratives to develop real or imagined experiences or events using effective techniques, well-chosen details, and well-structured event sequences.	**W.K.3:** Use a combination of drawing, dictating, and writing to narrate a single event or several loosely linked events, tell about the events in the order in which they occurred, and provide a reaction to what happened.	**W.1.3:** Write narratives in which they recount two or more appropriately sequenced events, include some details regarding what happened, use temporal words to signal event order, and provide some sense of closure.	**W.2.3:** Write narratives in which they recount a well-elaborated event or short sequence of events, include details to describe actions, thoughts, and feelings, use temporal words to signal event order, and provide a sense of closure.

Source: Adapted from NGA & CCSSO, 2010a, pp. 18–19.

The communicative intent of writing is apparent in kindergarten, as students use a combination of drawing and writing to express opinions, supply information, and tell a story. By first grade, these communications become more formal, especially through the use of concluding statements. In second grade, students use linking words in their opinion writing (for example, *because*), facts and definitions in their informative pieces, and details and signal words to suggest an order to their stories.

Text *type* should not be confused with writing *genre*. Students will encounter a multitude of genres in their literate lives. Specifically what constitutes a genre has been debated, but most people agree that there should be similarities in form, style, or subject matter for something to be called a genre (Coker, 2007; Kress, 1999; Miller, 1984; Short, Schroeder, Kauffman, & Kaser, 2004; Turbill & Bean, 2006). In other words, a genre has defining characteristics that are unique to a group of works. The genres students read may not be the genres that they learn to write, at least at grades K–2. For example, students may read westerns, science fiction, horror, fantasy, realistic fiction, poetry, and a host of other genres.

The Common Core State Standards identify three major text types: (1) opinion and persuasive, (2) informative and explanatory, and (3) narrative (NGA & CCSSO, 2010b). For each text type, there are specific genres that students should know and be able to use. Students are taught the characteristics of these genres so they can use these elements in their own writing. Skillful use of these elements allows the writer to convey ideas in a way the intended audience understands. Table 3.3 contains a summary of each text type and its genres, features, and writing characteristics.

Table 3.3: CCSS Text Types and Genres

Text Types	Genres	Features	Writing Characteristics
Opinion and Persuasive	Essay, speech, editorial, and letter to the editor	States an opinion or point of view and provides supporting reasons and information Seeks to convince a reader about the validity of a position or action	Defines a position Offers supporting evidence using primary and secondary sources Addresses concerns of the reader
Informative and Explanatory	Report of information, summary, and technical analysis and literary analysis	Conveys factual reports containing information or observations Briefly restates a text's main ideas Presents instructions and procedures	Uses multiple sources and documents sources Refrains from expressing opinions Identifies sequence accurately Uses correct format for document
Narrative	Autobiography, biography, creative fiction, and memoir	Uses time as a deep structure Has a narrator Establishes a situation and sequence	Informs, instructs, persuades, or entertains Uses monologue or dialogue, visual details, and actions

Source: Adapted from NGA & CCSSO, 2010b, pp. 23–24.

Opinion and Persuasive Writing

Everyone has an opinion but not everyone can support his or her opinion with reasons and information. Furthermore, not everyone can share his or her opinion in ways that encourage discussion about different viewpoints or use persuasive techniques to convince others about the argument. As students learn to share their opinions with others, they develop persuasive abilities. In opinion pieces and persuasive writing, students must support their point of view and eventually try to convince others to agree with the facts as presented, share values as outlined, accept specific arguments and conclusions, or adopt a way of thinking. Persuasive writing is often regarded as the most difficult for students to master. Students must commit to and sustain a line of reasoning and avoid introducing new topics within the paper. In addition, they need to demonstrate clear thinking through convincing argument, and ample credible evidence to support those statements. At the end of the piece, they must provide a conclusion that summarizes their logic and thinking. In grades K–2, this writing begins with students naming favorite events, items, and circumstances and making recommendations; by second grade, students are expected to connect their opinions to their reasons.

Informative and Explanatory Writing

A *factual report* conveys information or observations, often generically referred to as an *essay*. The purpose of this type of writing is to inform, not to persuade or react. It is commonly used in science and social studies contexts. Students must learn not to interject themselves or their opinions into this type of writing and instead use credible sources to support the facts they present. Typically, a factual report has a common structure that includes an opening paragraph that explains to readers what they will find in the paper, the body that leads the readers through the pertinent information, and a conclusion that summarizes the report's information. In other words, an informative or explanatory piece provides a forum for writers to report the information they have analyzed, summarize conclusions they have drawn from the information, consider alternatives to the information presented, and make a series of recommendations based on the information. In grades K–2, these can include (but are not limited to) *how-to* papers developed through shared writing, as well as short reports about science and social studies topics.

Narrative Writing

Students are also expected to write accounts of their lives and the lives of others, real or imagined. In our experience, students particularly like this text type. They enjoy reading about others and take pleasure in writing about themselves and people they find interesting. The key to writing good narratives is to collect enough information to tell a good story about the person, event, or experience. Students should learn to use descriptive language to capture the readers' interest and employ a variety of narrative techniques such as story grammar, dialogue, and literary devices. As students get older and become more skilled writers, they will be asked to produce papers in which they analyze a piece of literature or a poem. Typically, a series of questions guides their writing, such as:

- What happened in the story?
- What point do you think the author is making in the story?
- Do you think the story mirrors real life?

To respond to these types of questions, students need experience writing these responses, talking about literature, and receiving feedback. In grades K–2, these writing experiences include class compositions of familiar books that have been rewritten with original texts, as well as short stories told in narrative fashion.

Six second-grade students, Luis, Madeline, Bianca, Mark, Kristen, and Ann, approach the small-group instruction table and settle into their seats while their teacher, Vince Pham, distributes copies of a book they have read several times closely. The book, *Smoky Night* (Bunting, 1994), is a Caldecott award-winning story of a conflict between Daniel's cat and that of his neighbor Mrs. Kim. The backdrop is the Los Angeles riots, and the book ends with the pet owners reconsidering the importance of living together peacefully.

He distributes a rubric that he and his collaborative team developed to help students create friendly letters. He says, "We'll use this rubric to write a friendly letter from Daniel to Mrs. Kim. Let's imagine what he might say to her to encourage her to meet him. Remember that we have to honor what the text tells us." The group eagerly begins listing ideas for him to record. Madeline suggests, "Daniel needs to be very kind and say 'please' and 'thank you' a lot." Mark adds, "Maybe it would be easier to invite Mrs. Kim's cat as well because she would probably come if it was for the cats."

Mr. Pham then distributes a checklist of elements in a friendly letter and displays a language chart with a sample letter. The checklist includes the following seven items.

1. The date is at the top.
2. The greeting tells the person's name.
3. The first paragraph tells the letter's purpose.
4. The second paragraph is an invitation.
5. The third paragraph offers a thank-you.
6. The closing includes a short expression.
7. The letter ends with your signature.

Using the checklist, the students evaluate Mr. Pham's draft letter for necessary elements.

After Mr. Pham reminds the students to use the book to check for details to use in the letter, they begin writing. He observes each student as he or she writes, making notes about the student's progress. When he notices the students need help, he prompts them. For example, he helps Ann to get started with her writing. He asks Luis about the lack of details in his second paragraph when he notes that there is not information about where or when to meet. As each student finishes, he or she re-reads his or her letter with Mr. Pham and checks off the elements of a friendly letter. In the next lesson, the students read their letters to each other and use the rubric to check them.

Production and Distribution of Writing

This domain describes the procedural and technical aspects of writing (NGA & CCSSO, 2010a). Anchor standard four (W.CCR.4), which begins in grade 3, does not apply to students in grades K–2. Anchor standard five (W.CCR.5) foregrounds writing as a public and collaborative set of processes that require oral and written communicative skills and refers further to the Language standards as they relate to grammar and conventions of Standard English (these will be more fully explored in the next chapter). Finally, anchor standard six (W.CCR.6) extends the groundwork laid in the previous standard by defining the public space beyond the classroom and into digital environments. Table 3.4 presents the anchor standards and the grade-level standards. This represents a shift in how writing is taught. The technical skills of keyboarding and word processing need to be viewed as basic skills, in the same way that we view holding a pencil correctly. Sure, it's important for a time, but it's not our endpoint. No one would confuse pencil grip with written communication; we should not confound operating a word-processing program with writing, either.

Table 3.4: Writing Standards for Domain Production and Distribution of Writing, Grades K–2

Anchor Standards	Kindergarten Standards	Grade 1 Standards	Grade 2 Standards
W.CCR.4: Produce clear and coherent writing in which the development, organization, and style are appropriate to the task, audience, and purpose.	n/a	n/a	n/a
W.CCR.5: Develop and strengthen writing as needed by planning, revising, editing, rewriting, or trying a new approach.	**W.K.5:** With guidance and support from adults, respond to questions and suggestions from peers and add details to strengthen writing as needed.	**W.1.5:** With guidance and support from adults, focus on a topic, respond to questions and suggestions from peers, and add details to strengthen writing as needed.	**W.2.5:** With guidance and support from adults and peers, focus on a topic and strengthen writing as needed by revising and editing.
W.CCR.6: Use technology, including the Internet, to produce and publish writing and to interact and collaborate with others.	**W.K.6:** With guidance and support from adults, explore a variety of digital tools to produce and publish writing, including in collaboration with peers.	**W.1.6:** With guidance and support from adults, use a variety of digital tools to produce and publish writing, including in collaboration with peers.	**W.2.6:** With guidance and support from adults, use a variety of digital tools to produce and publish writing, including in collaboration with peers.

Source: Adapted from NGA & CCSSO, 2010a, pp. 18–19.

These first two domains in the writing anchor standards—(1) Text Types and (2) Production and Distribution—reset our vision of what writing should be. It's not the *tools* of writing as much as it is the *functions*: we find, use, produce, and share information (Frey, Fisher, & Gonzalez, 2010). Young writers will encounter tools we can't even imagine at this point in the history of the information era, but if sufficiently equipped with a deep understanding of the functions of writing, they can adopt these new tools more quickly and more fully. Carol Elliot's first-grade class regularly uses digital tools to explore these functions. For example, her students produce and share their writing using the digital storyboard website VoiceThread (www.voicethread.com).

Ms. Elliot explains, "The best feature is that other students can leave comments, ask questions, and add information through text boxes or audio recordings. I type and record their original poems and reports, and students and I can ask and respond to questions. For instance, we had been writing poems with rhyming words, and I ask students to identify the rhymes in their classmate's poems. They use a digital tool to circle the words on the screen and get to see their classmates do the same."

The public and collaborative nature of writing requires that students see themselves as both readers and writers. They are readers of published works, of course, but they are also readers of each other's writing. In addition, writers need to understand the importance of audience in shaping their writing. As students write longer pieces, they need to find out what a reader understands. This is consistent with the practices of professional writers, who seek the feedback of an editor to refine their work. Peer response allows students to come together as fellow writers to read each other's work and give constructive feedback. Peer response is not peer editing or peer teaching. Peer response is discussion between a writer and a reader about the ideas in a piece and how they are understood. The teacher, and only the teacher, is responsible for editing and the feedback that goes with it. Novice writers lack the ability to edit sufficiently well for it to be helpful, and they lack the communication skills to negotiate these conversations. In addition, there are essential conditions regarding when and how teachers utilize peer response. If students are not yet experiencing success as writers, then peer response may not be appropriate. As students become comfortable with writing, and are producing text, teachers can introduce peer response, which helps writers see the connection to their audience and receive feedback about their messages. General guidelines for using peer response include the following.

- The writer determines when he or she needs peer feedback.
- The teacher and students recognize that not all writing needs peer feedback.
- Teachers, not students, should offer editing feedback on the details of the piece.
- Students should provide feedback that is focused on a reader's needs and a writer's strategies.

These guidelines are useful reminders that the writer decides when he or she is ready for peer feedback. Few things are more dispiriting than receiving criticism about a piece the writer knows is not ready for review. This can serve to discourage the writer and prevent him or her from seeking peer responses in the future. Peer response functions best in a classroom environment that is conducive to communication and in which experimentation is expected and honored.

Some peer responses are less helpful and can even be harmful to young writers. In particular, global praise does little to provide the writer with any feedback that might be useful. Additionally, feedback that focuses on word- and sentence-level editing mirrors what the teacher often does and may not be welcome by fellow students. Rather, the purpose of seeking peer responses is not to have the work evaluated but to hear what a reader understood and where the reader became confused (Simmons, 2003).

Once teachers instruct students on the types of appropriate responses, students can use a simple peer response form to give back to the writer. It is helpful for writers to receive comments in writing so they have an idea of what to do next. The teacher should review these peer comments in order to monitor whether students are offering helpful responses. Figure 3.2 is an example of a peer response form.

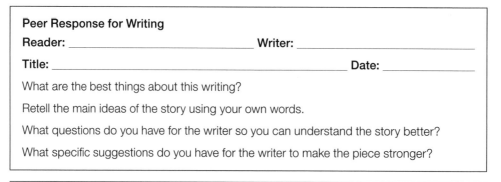

Figure 3.2: Peer response feedback form.

Visit **go.solution-tree.com/commoncore** for a reproducible version of this figure.

Teachers can prepare posters to guide students in their conversations with peers about writing. For example, students can refer to the posters—"How Fellow Writers Talk" and "How Fellow Writers Listen"—to help their conversation.

How Fellow Writers Talk

1. Tell your fellow writer what you liked best.
2. Retell the story or main ideas in your own words.
3. Ask questions about the parts you don't understand.
4. Give your fellow writer your good ideas about making it even better.
5. Thank the writer for sharing his or her writing with you.

How Fellow Writers Listen

1. Listen to the ideas your fellow writer offers.
2. Ask questions about ideas you don't understand.
3. Thank your fellow writer for reading your writing.
4. Use the ideas you like in your writing.

Visit **go.solution-tree.com/commoncore** for a reproducible version of these feature boxes.

Research to Build and Present Knowledge

Anchor standards seven and eight (W.CCR.7 and W.CCR.8) in this domain set students on a writing path they will use throughout the remainder of their school and work lives: the ability to report experiences and information (see table 3.5). Anchor standard seven introduces short collaboratively written research projects to kindergarten students, through introductory experiences with co-constructed inquiry-based projects in the primary grades. In kindergarten, these take the form of author studies; while in first grade, they expand to how-to writing. By second grade, students are co-writing short reports on a single topic, such as a science report. Unlike anchor standards seven and eight, anchor standard nine (W.CCR.9) does not apply to students in grades K–2: it begins in fourth grade.

Table 3.5: Writing Standards for Domain Research to Build and Present Knowledge, Grades K–2

Anchor Standards	Kindergarten Standards	Grade 1 Standards	Grade 2 Standards
W.CCR.7: Conduct short as well as more sustained research projects based on focused questions, demonstrating understanding of the subject under investigation.	**W.K.7:** Participate in shared research and writing projects (such as explore a number of books by a favorite author and express opinions about them).	**W.1.7:** Participate in shared research and writing projects (such as explore a number of how-to books on a given topic and use them to write a sequence of instructions).	**W.2.7:** Participate in shared research and writing projects (such as read a number of books on a single topic to produce a report; record science observations).
W.CCR.8: Gather relevant information from multiple print and digital sources, assess the credibility and accuracy of each source, and integrate the information while avoiding plagiarism.	**W.K.8:** With guidance and support from adults, recall information from experiences or gather information from provided sources to answer a question.	**W.1.8:** With guidance and support from adults, recall information from experiences or gather information from provided sources to answer a question.	**W.2.8:** Recall information from experiences or gather information from provided sources to answer a question.
W.CCR.9: Draw evidence from literary or informational texts to support analysis, reflection, and research.	n/a	n/a	n/a

Source: Adapted from NGA & CCSSO, 2010a, pp. 18–19.

Anchor standard eight (W.CCR.8) highlights the importance of organizing information during research, especially in making useful notes that can be utilized during the writing process. A student's ability to take and organize notes is a significant predictor of success.

A Focus on Annotation and Note Taking

Over time, and with instruction, students not only use their notes for externally storing information but also for encoding their ideas. This builds comprehension and understanding of the content (Ganske, 1981). Note taking is also a critical skill for college success (Pauk, 1974), so it's an important skill to master early on. Notes help students quickly find information, locate references, participate in shared research and writing projects, and "recall information from experiences or gather information from provided sources to answer a question" (W.K.8, W.1.8, and W.2.8; NGA & CCSSO, 2010a, p. 19).

In their seminal text *How to Read a Book*, Mortimer Adler and Charles Van Doren (1972) lay out a case for engaging in repeated readings with accompanying annotation:

> Why is marking a book indispensable to reading it? First, it keeps you awake not merely conscious, but wide awake. Second, reading, if active, is thinking, and thinking tends to express itself in words, spoken or written. The person who says he knows what he thinks but cannot express it usually does not know what he thinks. Third, writing your reactions down helps you remember the thoughts of the author. (p. 49)

Additionally, Susan Vanneman (2011) suggests that note taking is as easy as ABC LOU, a mnemonic device that stands for *abbreviations, bullets, caveman language, lists, one word for several*, and *use your own words*. Using annotations and using mnemonics are just a couple ways students can take quick but efficient notes.

Other Note-Taking Methods

Of course, there are other ways for students to take notes. In the primary grades, students can take group notes through interactive writing events (Frey & Fisher, 2007b). This may involve a group of students talking about a text and then sharing the pen to create their notes. The key for teachers is to instruct students to extract meaningful information and record the sources. Daniel Callison and Leslie Preddy (2006) identify four note-taking strategies for web pages: (1) highlight key terms and statements, (2) write a summary, (3) recite information learned, and (4) cite the source. Regardless of the format, students should learn the five Rs of note taking: (1) record meaningful facts and ideas; (2) reduce the text to main ideas and summaries; (3) recite the most important terms, concepts, ideas, and conclusions; (4) reflect on personal opinion and perspective; and (5) review.

Robin McCarthy's first graders are involved in an extended study comparing the past with the present. They are reading books from Robin Nelson's *Then and Now* series, which features topics ranging from communication to home, transportation, school, and games and toys. As part of their experiences in developing opinions supported with evidence from the text and their own thinking, the students read *Transportation: Then and Now* (Nelson, 2003). As a class, the students chart the differences that the author identifies, returning to the text several times to discuss what they found. For example, early in the book there is a picture of a couple in a horse-drawn carriage, and the text reads, "Transportation has changed over time" (p. 3). Duane says, "We should add the horse to the past." Julie asks "Why? We still have horses now." Brian says, "Yeah, but people go in cars now, not like that [*pointing to the carriage*]." Mary agrees, saying, "That looks like a long time ago, not now."

In this unit, students are expected to form an opinion and identify a reason for their opinion. Ms. McCarthy wants students to identify one thing from the past that they wish they still had and one thing that they are glad to have now. As students prepare to write, Ms. McCarthy reminds them that they have to provide a rationale for their opinions. "Remember, it's not enough to tell your reader what you wish you had from the past, but to tell them *why* you wish you had it."

Cody writes, "I wish we still had covered wagons because it would be fun to ride in."

Amanda writes, "I would like streetcars from the past. They would be better than the bus because they are open up on the side for air to get in." Lauren writes, "We should travel in ships now because they could take a lot of people."

These students are learning to use evidence from the text, form an opinion, and support that opinion. This is a very important skill to teach and develop if students are to eventually become persuasive speakers and writers who can convince others of their ideas. As we will discuss in greater detail in chapter 4 on the strands Speaking and Listening and Language, sentence frames can be used to guide students into academic writing. (See chapter 5, page 143, for more information about sentence frames.) In terms of forming an opinion, the following frames are helpful.

- I agree/disagree with _____ because _____ .
- They say _____ and/but I say _____ because _____ .
- I agree with _____ (source) that _____ (opinion/perspective) because _____ .
- From the perspective of _____ , I think/understand _____ .

Over time, these frames become part of students' writing habits, and they use them automatically while modifying the words to address the audience and topic (Fisher & Frey, 2007b).

Range of Writing

Anchor standard ten (W.CCR.10) is intended to provide students a chance to write and discuss their writing with others. This standard is not formally applied until grade 3 although teachers in grades K–2 can and should provide students opportunities to write independently. This can occur as part of the literacy block when students are writing journal entries, lists, and letters and summarizing their experiences. In addition, Maria Paula Ghiso (2011) reminds us that students should be invited to write about what matters to them. This allows them to see that their words are powerful and serves to motivate young writers to write more and better.

The Writing Process

As with other strands in the Common Core State Standards, writing doesn't isolate one standard while ignoring others within or across strands. Young writers require ongoing multidimensional instruction that fulfills the expectations of the CCSS. Interactive and personal writing experiences enable students to grow in their understanding of what they need to do to write well. Teachers model writing behavior in shared and guided writing activities during which students take turns contributing ideas, dictating words or sentences, or transcribing the message. As students observe writing and participate in the development of a piece, they become aware of appropriate writing behaviors and can begin to apply what they have observed to their personal and independent writing. As students develop proficiency in writing, they become aware of the attributes of good writers.

- Good writers know effective habits of writing will increase the efficiency and quality of their writing. Young writers need to learn how to organize materials, how to utilize reference materials to support content, and what skills they need to get their ideas down on paper.

- Good writers know how to move from ideas to words to sentences and paragraphs. The less adept writer will be frustrated with his or her inability to transmit ideas to the reader. Writing craft includes word choice, perspective, and recognizing that different genres require different approaches.

- Good writers use punctuation, spelling, and grammatical structures to ensure that readers understand their message. Selecting the correct genre of writing to fit the purpose goes hand in hand with the conventions associated with clear writing.

Aspects of the Writing Process

Good writers understand that there is a process to writing and that their awareness of the process can facilitate writing. Writing teacher and researcher Donald Graves (personal communication as cited in Nagin, 2003) writes:

> The writing process is anything a writer does from the time the idea came until the piece is completed or abandoned. There is no particular order. So it's not effective to teach writing process in a lock-step, rigid manner. What a good writing teacher does is help students see where writing comes from; in a chance remark or an article that really burns you up. I still hold by my original statement: if kids don't write more than three days a week they're dead, and it's very hard to become a writer. If you provide frequent occasions for writing then the students start to think about writing when they're not doing it. I call it a constant state of composition. (p. 23)

While we do not advocate for a strictly sequential approach to writing that moves students through a lockstep system, we do believe that students will benefit from learning common writing techniques. Five common writing dimensions are the following.

1. **Prewriting:** Formulating (or brainstorming) ideas that may or may not be utilized later in a writing piece

2. **Drafting:** Committing brainstormed ideas to paper to produce a first draft

3. **Revising:** Revisiting the draft to add, delete, or change what has been drafted

4. **Editing:** Approaching the piece's final form and asking teachers or peers for corrections and feedback on content

5. **Publishing:** Finalizing the piece and sharing it with others

These dimensions build on one another to contribute to the writer's growing stamina and fluency in order *to get in the zone*. If you like sports, you know what it means to be *in the zone*. Athletes in the zone report feeling that time is suspended and that their movements are fluid. Similarly, some people report *getting lost* in a book or good movie. Mihaly Csikszentmihalyi (1997) calls this phenomenon *flow*. He believes that flow is an optimal experience for humans. Fluent writers also gain a sense of flow as they write.

The Characteristics of Flow

In simple terms, Csikszentmihalyi's research suggests that people are generally unhappy doing nothing, happy doing things, and uncertain about what makes them happy. However, people fully engaged in a task *get lost* in the activity or *get in the zone* or what he likes to call *flow*. According to Csikszentmihalyi (1997), there are a number of characteristics of flow, which include the following.

- **Complete involvement, focus, and concentration:** Being innately curious or as the result of having training

- **A sense of ecstasy:** Being outside everyday reality

- **A great inner clarity:** Knowing what needs to be done and how well it is going

- **Knowledge that the activity is doable:** Knowing that one's skills are adequate and that the task does not create anxiety or boredom

- **A sense of serenity:** Not worrying about self; feeling of growing beyond the boundaries of ego—afterward feeling of transcending ego in ways not thought possible

- **Timeliness:** Thoroughly focusing on the present; not noticing time passing

- **Intrinsic motivation:** Using whatever produces flow as a reward

Source: Adapted from Csikszentmihalyi, 1997.

As you can imagine, a goal of teachers is to keep students in flow for as much of the school day as possible. Csikszentmihalyi (1997, 2000) notes, humans cannot be in flow all of the time—it is an optimal state, not necessarily a common state of being. When the challenge is relatively high and skills are relatively low, students become anxious. Importantly, when the challenge is relatively low and skills are relatively high, students become bored. When both are low, a profound sense of apathy is apparent.

We believe that flow is influenced in part by fluency in reading and writing. Not being able to read smoothly and accurately is frustrating, causes anxiety, and results in poor comprehension. The message the brain processes becomes halting, choppy, and disjointed. A similar phenomenon occurs with disfluent writing. When ideas are coming faster than one can write, students become frustrated. If they do not have good command of spelling and vocabulary, they oversimplify their sentences with low-level words and ideas, or give up altogether on their writing. Alternatively, smooth and accurate reading allows the reader to concentrate on the meaning of the message, an important contributor to motivation and interest. Likewise, the ability to compose a message without having to stop after every word to recall spelling or syntax allows the writer to concentrate on more sophisticated writing behaviors, such as planning, composing, and revising to create the best message. Without a doubt, fluency in reading and writing is important because it contributes to the learner's ability to fully engage with the literacy activity.

Aspects of Writing Fluency

Writing fluency has received significantly less research attention compared with reading fluency. However, it stands to reason that not writing quickly enough would be frustrating for students. Imagine having all kinds of ideas in your head, but having them leave you before you can record them! Similarly, poor writing volume results in few words to edit. After all, if a student only generates a few dozen words after fifteen minutes of writing, he or she will not have much to edit and revise. Most importantly, a focus on writing fluency requires that students move on with the task of writing and not procrastinate. We've all watched a student staring off into space after being asked to respond in writing to a question or comment. When asked, this student will respond, "I'm thinking" or "I'm not sure what to write." A focus on writing fluency provides students with the skills to record their thoughts, supplies them with ideas to edit and revise, and addresses the frequent delays associated with writing performance. (See pages 84–86 for sample activities to focus on writing fluency.)

While there are a number of theories about writing and how to write, writers generally use three interactive and recursive components: "*planning* what to say, *translating* those plans into written text, and *reviewing* those written texts or plans" (McCutcheon, Covill, Hoyne, & Mildes, 1994, p. 256). We maintain that a focus on writing fluency requires attention to each of these three components.

Planning the Message

During planning students must develop the skills to rapidly organize their thinking and develop a scheme for their ideas. Naturally there are a number of strategies that focus on this component, including brainstorming ideas, talking to a partner, thinking and searching through texts, and developing concept maps.

Translating the Message

As students translate their plans into text, they must have developed the motor skills for extended writing tasks, have the stamina to write for extended periods, and be able to make connections between what they've written and what they're thinking. Predictably, there are specific instructional routines to help students develop this component, including quick writes, freewrites, timed writings, and power writing. (See pages 84–86 for more information on these instructional strategies.)

Reviewing the Message

In terms of reviewing, students need to be able to read what they've written and revise accordingly. Again, it's important to note that writing is recursive and interactive—writers revise as they write and think as they revise and so on. We encourage young writers to read their writing aloud so they can locate errors or omissions.

Muschla (1993) suggests that all students be taught a simple five-step plan for revision.

1. Read the piece silently and then aloud. Reading it aloud can highlight the flow and rhythm of the words.
2. Consider the whole piece first. What are its strengths? What parts do you like best? What are its weaknesses? How can the weaknesses be improved? What can be added? What can be eliminated?
3. Focus on the paragraphs. Are they well organized? Does each have a main idea supported by details? Do the paragraphs follow each other logically? Are the transitions between them smooth?
4. Consider the sentences. Do they follow logically? Are they clear?
5. Focus on the words and phrases. Which should be changed? What are examples of clutter? (pp. 62–63)

There is no expected writing fluency rate that can provide teachers guidance with determining how many words per minute students should be able to write. However, writing fluency does appear to have a significant effect on a young child's ability to write. A large study of students at the end of kindergarten finds that their oral language skills, spelling, and especially letter-writing fluency are strong contributors to an emergent writer's ability to produce original text (Kim et al., 2011). The children in the study average sixteen words in a fifteen-minute timed writing sample, but the range is wide: some children produce no words during that time, while the most fluent writer writes 139 words. Interestingly, the researchers find that reading level is not an especially strong predictor at this age. At some point, fluency is sufficient and further attempts to increase written production will compromise the writing quality. The point is that students need practice getting their ideas on paper such that they have content to edit and revise.

Fluency and Writing Maturity

As with reading, writing fluency is not only about writing more words. As students become more fluent writers, they also become more sophisticated writers. V. Andree Bayliss and Nancy Walker (1988) and Bayliss (1994) identify signs of maturing writing fluency, including:

- Providing details
- Elaborating on the subject
- Varying sentence patterns
- Deepening and unfolding the presentation
- Sustaining focus

As writers become more fluent, they are able to use these devices to produce more sophisticated pieces of writing. When a writer adds detail, the reader can visualize the setting and characters. Elaboration on a subject helps the reader to more fully understand what the writer is discussing (the sentences in this paragraph are examples of elaboration). As well, a mature writer can deepen and unfold a presentation by building on concepts in a logical manner. Finally, a good writer does not wander from topic to topic. Taken together, these characteristics form the definition of good writing and an effective writer. Think back to our description of the characteristics of a self-extending writer (page 66). Educators in grades K–2 play an important role in establishing the foundations students will need to become mature writers.

Writing fluency is important in the primary classroom because it contributes to more sophisticated expression of ideas. Reading fluency contributes to more sophisticated understanding of ideas. Neither reading nor writing fluency exist in isolation, but rather are influenced by a learner's control of phonics, syntax, comprehension, and vocabulary. However, fluency serves as an important bridge between these processes. Instruction in reading and writing fluency contributes to improving literacy skills of students.

Power Writing

Power writing is a daily instructional routine to build writing fluency. It involves brief, timed writing events. Leif Fearn and Nancy Farnan (2001) describe it as "a structured free-write where the objective is quantity alone" (p. 501). Teachers can begin to use power writing in the middle of first grade. Typically, this exercise is performed daily in three rounds of timed writing events, each one minute in length. Students are given a word or phrase to use somewhere in their writing and are reminded to "write as much as you can, as well as you can" (Fearn & Farnan, 2001, p. 196). At the end of one minute, they count the number of words they have written and note the total in the margin. This cycle is repeated two more times using different words or phrases. After the last cycle, they re-read what they have written and circle words they believe they may have misspelled. This allows the teacher to evaluate students' self-monitoring of their spelling. They keep a graph where they list the highest number of words for the day.

The purpose of tracking progress is not to establish a competitive atmosphere; these graphs are kept in the writer's notebook, which only the teacher or student views. These simple charts can be constructed on graph paper. See figure 3.3 for a sample graph. The words per minute are recorded on the vertical axis and should begin with a number that is just below the writer's current range of words. The teacher establishes this value

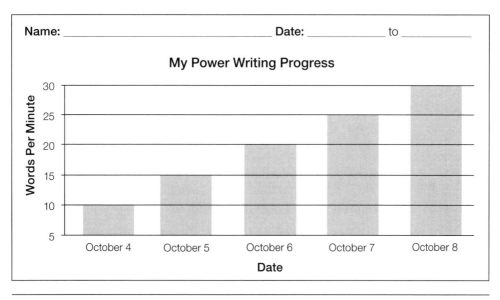

Figure 3.3: Sample power writing graph.

Visit **go.solution-tree.com/commoncore** for a reproducible version of this figure.

based on the student's power writing average and his or her goal for each student. For instance, if a writer currently averages ten words per minute, the vertical axis might begin with five.

Students completing three sessions of power writing are likely to observe another unexpected benefit. Typically, performance increases between the first and third rotation. By assessing their own progress, students internalize their own motivation as they seek to improve on their last effort. This is especially important for struggling writers, who commonly say that they "don't know what to write about." If they are stuck, they should be instructed to write the prompt word repeatedly until an idea formulates. As they do so, they begin to think of related words and often start to generate an idea, even if it is only a list of words at the start.

Journal Writing

An effective instructional program provides many opportunities for children to write across subjects and throughout the school day and week. As Graves notes, "If you provide frequent occasions for writing then the students start to think about writing when they're not doing it" (personal communication as cited in Nagin, 2003, p. 23). To help children observe and appreciate their growth as writers, we believe that every student should have a place to keep his or her writing. This is often accomplished through the use of a writing journal. Although organization of the writer's notebook varies by teacher, grade level, and purpose, most are arranged chronologically. Therefore, the various writing exercises done during shared, guided, and collaborative writing are likely to be in there. We recommend devoting a section of the notebook to fluency exercises like power writing. During independent writing, we sometimes invite students to review past power writing work in the journal and select one to expand into a more finished piece. Students frequently discover a good idea that they had previously overlooked.

The students in Marla Gomez's first-grade classroom use their writer's notebooks as a tool for conferring with their teacher about their writing progress. Having read *Don't Let the Pigeon Drive the Bus!* (Willems, 2003) several times, Ms. Gomez uses the selection as the basis for a writing lesson. She writes the following prompts on the board.

- The pigeon is . . .
- This story reminds me of when . . .
- I think the author wrote this story because . . .
- I would recommend this story to . . .

Students discuss the sentence stems and then compose their responses in their notebooks. This gives them experience at listening to others and considering new ideas. As they compose and discuss their ideas, Ms. Gomez invites Jeremy to meet with her. Jeremy has difficulty composing, and Ms. Gomez knows that he needs additional support. She asks Jeremy to share his first sentence, and he says, "The pigeon is trying to steal it." Ms. Gomez asks, "Steal what?" Jeremy replies, "The bus!" Ms. Gomez suggests that he include that in his sentence because "people who read your sentence later, like your mom, might not have read the book and will need for you to be very clear."

As the students complete the task, Ms. Gomez invites several students to share, reminding them that their responses need to include evidence from the text. Kelly offers, "I think that the author wrote this story because he wanted to make us laugh. I think that because he makes the pigeon look funny on this page [*pointing to pp. 21–22*]."

Freewriting

Students also need time to write for their own purposes and should be encouraged to write for their own motivation. We return to the concept we discussed earlier—*flow*. Peter Elbow (1981) describes a process called *freewriting* as a method for opening creative pathways. For ten minutes a day, students write independently on a topic of their own choice. During this time, no editing takes place. The sole purpose is to get words down on paper. This differs somewhat from power writing in that it is not viewed as a competition against the clock but rather as a way of accessing ideas. When stuck, writers are instructed to write anything—even squiggles—until the words come again. Sometimes the squiggles give the brain a little time to focus and produce. If a student struggles with language, the teacher may need to meet individually with him or her to develop some ideas collaboratively that can be used in future writing sessions. Freewriting can be valuable for students to tap into their understanding of the world and themselves.

What About Early Kindergarten Writing?

Previously we discussed the importance of daily writing as a means to build fluency in formulating ideas, transcribing messages, and reviewing one's writing. However, most children enter kindergarten with little or no experience at writing. Yet by the end of the school year, most are writing. It is wondrous to watch literacy blossom. Kindergarteners' ability to write begins with many shared experiences with writing.

Language experience approach (LEA) uses a child's language to create original text for reading (Ashton-Warner, 1965; Stauffer, 1970). LEA capitalizes on a child's language patterns to create materials to read and eventually to write. In most LEA lessons, the teacher records exactly what the child says. Teachers may be tempted to correct errors in grammar and syntax, but the point is to create text students can then read back. When the language is familiar, the likelihood of being able to do so is successfully increased. Shared experience is an essential basis for language experience approach, as the students need to have a common bank of knowledge to participate. This means that the teacher must first attend to creating experiences for students to discuss.

Creating Experiences

Experience is an operative word in LEA and is key to successful LEA lessons. Some students may not have experienced a particular event and thus are unable to offer language about the topic. Imagine, for instance, how difficult it would be for you to discuss the Fourth of July if you had never seen or celebrated the holiday. Therefore, teachers often create a shared experience with the class in order to use the event later in an LEA lesson. Field trips and school activities are ideally suited for this because all the students have participated and can talk about their experience when they return to the classroom. Some of these events lead to unexpected conversations. For example, when Nancy took her class on a disastrous field trip that included a severe thunderstorm, a leaking bus roof, and a driver who lost the keys, the shared experience became a class book titled, *The Terrible, Horrible, No Good, Very Bad Field Trip!*

Creating Text

As stated earlier, the purpose of an LEA lesson is to capture the natural language of children. This is accomplished through establishing a purpose for the writing and initiating a conversation to fulfill the stated purpose. Sometimes referred to as *authentic writing*, the goal is to create a purpose for the writing that is viewed as meaningful for the students, not just the teacher. Many students respond to a purpose associated with the permanence of the written product. For example, daily class news and bound books are both popular choices.

Daily class news is constructed to report on the events that occur within the classroom community. While these events may appear mundane to the outsider, they are often of great interest to the students. Topics can range from the lunch menu to classroom visitors and academic activities. The importance of composing the daily class news has less to do with the topic than the composing and writing experience itself. Effective daily class news writing requires the following five steps.

1. Do it every day.

2. Date each entry.

3. Make sure the students can clearly see what is being written as it is being written.

4. Re-read the entry several times with the class.

5. Make the composition easily available for future reading.

Class books serve as another purpose for LEA lessons. These are small or large in size and contain the original written text composed with the students. Remember that LEA relies on preserving the language of the students, so resist the urge to edit. Like the daily class news, class books should be written so that all students can see the print being developed on the page. Photographs or illustrations may be added later to the text, but it is not an absolute. The emphasis is not on turning out elaborately bound and laminated works of art. Many of these class books are simply stapled sheaves of papers. The real value of these class books is that the students generate text they can practice reading because it is in their natural language. Over time, children begin creating their own texts.

Conclusion

Learning to write is not a matter of simply brainstorming, drafting, editing, revising, and publishing. It's much messier than that and occasionally (if we are very lucky) reaches a state of flow. Our efforts to foster young writers are focused on enabling them to move closer to that *constant state of composition*. In order for students to become writers who are adept at using different text types, and with different purposes and audiences in mind, they must write throughout the day. If they are to produce and distribute their writing across the classroom and the world, they must write frequently. If students are to engage in research in order to build their knowledge and present it to others, they must write across disciplines. Simply stated, writing needs to be part of the air that is breathed in every classroom.

Writing is a time when students are provided an opportunity to apply the skills they have been learning to create original texts. Students write for a variety of purposes and have a voice in the choice of topics and in making editing decisions. The type of writing a student engages in is influenced by the developmental level of the student and the purpose for writing. The core standards for writing highlight the importance of writing as a communicative channel across disciplines. Like other aspects of the core standards, writing should not be confined to the literacy block, but should be incorporated across the learning day.

As with the Reading standards, the Writing standards build on content teachers already know. Writing is a major facet of students' schooling, but the question we have to ask ourselves is, are they getting any better at writing? Research evidence from large-scale writing assessments such as the National Assessment of Educational Progress suggests that there is still a lot of work to be done in this area (Salahu-Din, Persky, & Miller, 2008). Overall, the writing that students do in school is not sufficient for them to be successful in college and careers. Rather than assign writing or tell students to write, teachers have to focus on writing *instruction*. This is where your K–2 collaborative planning team can help. As we have noted throughout this chapter, teams can focus their planning conversations around three questions.

1. **Standards:** What is the essence of this standard?

2. **Instruction:** What teacher actions facilitate this standard in practice?

3. **Formative assessment:** What evidence that students are learning this standard will we accept?

By focusing on these questions, teams will develop a scope and sequence of writing curriculum that is connected with the reading students are doing. Teams will also ensure that writing is integrated into the speaking and listening activities students engage in and that language development is occurring so students can write increasingly sophisticated pieces. As we have noted, the Common Core State Standards are interconnected. The writing standards must be taught in the context of all of the other standards so student competence and confidence are routinely raised.

CHAPTER 4

Implementing the Common Core State Standards for Speaking and Listening and for Language

KEY QUESTIONS

• To what extent does your team understand the Speaking and Listening standards and the Language standards? What is our current level of knowledge about this standard? How can we increase our expertise? How will we measure our growth?

• How much classroom speaking do students do that is academic in nature? Do they use argumentation and provide evidence for their claims when they share their thinking?

• How sophisticated is the language that students use in speaking and writing? Are there language structures that students need to learn to be successful?

Linda Martinez-Garza is leading her second-grade mathematics students in a lesson on fluently and flexibly grouping by tens and fives. She is using *One Hundred Hungry Ants* (Pinczes, 1993) as a shared reading. The book has a quantitative measure of AD650L, which means that the book is intended to be used as an adult-directed book. Ms. Martinez-Garza has read and discussed the book previously with her students. Now they are ready to explore the mathematical concepts that form the heart of the story. Using interlocking counting cubes, her students are working in groups of two or three to replicate the ants' formations. Importantly, this activity requires that students collaborate in order to correctly set up the cubes. She reviews the class norms for productive group work, which are the following.

• Listen carefully when others are speaking.

• Ask questions when you don't understand something.

• Give a reason why your idea is a good one.

• Use ideas from others to make your group's ideas even better.

She reads the first four pages, invites the students to assemble the one hundred counting cubes into one long lines and asks them to notice the length of a single-file line of one hundred ants.

"It would take them too long to get to the picnic!" Ricky offers, recalling the problem in the story. "That's right! So let's look at how they try to solve this problem," Ms. Martinez-Garza replies.

After reading the "littlest ant's" suggestion to line up in two groups of fifty, Angelica's group sets to work. "We have to make these into two piles," she says, and Paolo quickly offers, "But let's keep them locked together, because otherwise they'll go everywhere." Simon nods. "That's a good idea. I'll make one pile, and you can make the other." Angelica joins in, "I'll write the math problem [*gesturing to the group's whiteboard*] so we'll be ready."

Exchanges like this occur in groups throughout the room. In a matter of minutes, the students have experimented with different grouping arrangements—four groups of twenty-five and five groups of twenty. As they reach the end of the story, Ms. Martinez-Garza poses one more question. "Here's the challenge problem for your teams. Can you find one more way to regroup, and tell us why you did it?" The three students try different arrangements to no avail, until Paolo has an idea. "We could break these lines in two [*gesturing to the groups of twenty cubes*] and then we'd have . . . [*begins counting*] ten!" says Angelica. "We're a good team!"

Ms. Martinez-Garza's lesson is an example of the interconnectedness of the CCSS ELA and the CCSS for mathematics. The mathematics task of grouping by hundreds and fives expects students to meet standards in the grade 2 mathematics content standard domains Operations and Algebraic Thinking and Number and Operations in Base Ten (see NGA & CCSSO, 2010e, p. 19). Furthermore, the activity calls on students to use two of the CCSS Mathematical Practices: Mathematical Practice 4, Model with mathematics, and Mathematical Practice 5, Use appropriate tools strategically (NGA & CCSSO, 2010e, p. 7).

A Collaborative Planning Team in Action

It should come as no surprise that the unit of instruction Ms. Martinez-Garza developed for *One Hundred Hungry Ants* began with her collaborative planning team's conversations about the Common Core State Standards for English language arts and the CCSS for mathematics. Grouping for place value is a challenging concept for second graders, and the team knew that having the students working together on this topic was critical. The teachers' efforts across grades K–2 have been on building the speaking and listening skills of their students in order to engage in collaborative learning. "For us, the key to understanding the Speaking and Listening standards was to overlay them onto every other aspect of the curriculum," Ms. Martinez-Garza offers. "It made no sense to think we could teach these skills in isolation. For our collaborative planning team, these two sets of standards are the *go-to* ones we look at each time we plan." She continues,

"But we needed to build our own knowledge before we could ever hope to build that of our students." In order to analyze the core standards in depth, the team focuses on three overarching questions.

1. What is our current level of knowledge about this standard?

2. How can we increase our expertise?

3. How will we measure our growth?

Figure 4.1 (pages 94–95) and figure 4.2 (pages 96–97) offer sample protocols you can use in your collaborative team to analyze the Speaking and Listening and Language standards, using the three guiding questions from Ms. Martinez-Garza and her collaborative team. (Visit **go.solution-tree.com/commoncore** for online-only reproducibles of these figures.)

Because the Speaking and Listening strand and the Language strand are interrelated, we will examine them together in this chapter. Language is not confined only to the oral and verbal domains: it supports them. Like Ms. Martinez-Garza's collaborative planning team, we hope that you and your collaborative team will use this approach to ensure that these standards are integral to all your lessons. In other words, when planning lessons, collaborative teams should not focus only on one strand, be that Reading, Writing, Speaking and Listening, or Language. Instead, they should identify opportunities to address appropriate standards from each area. Similarly, team members should consider how the standards apply across the curriculum.

Anchor Standards for Speaking and Listening

The anchor standards for Speaking and Listening spotlight the quality of transactions students have across the table, classroom, and world. NGA and CCSSO (2010a) note, "Students must have ample opportunities to take part in a variety of rich, structured conversations—as part of a whole class, in small groups, and with a partner" (p. 22). In the 21st century, in which digital communications have become a feature of everyday life, these communication skills extend to virtual environments. These anchor standards are divided into two domains: (1) Comprehension and Collaboration, and (2) Presentation of Knowledge and Ideas. Together, they outline the expectations for the informal and formal talk of an effective classroom. Notice how these standards clearly link to those discussed in Reading and Writing strands in chapters 2 and 3.

Comprehension and Collaboration

The three anchor standards in this domain focus on the students' growing ability to collaborate with others in a meaningful way, using the content as the platform for their work. Anchor standard one (SL.CCR.1) describes the dispositions of the student who is prepared to fully participate in academic discussions. Anchor standard three (SL.CCR.3) is reminiscent of the work on accountable talk, which describes the habits of speakers and listeners as they engage in academic discourse, such as incorporating the statements

Speaking and Listening anchor standard one (SL.CCR.1): Prepare for and participate effectively in a range of conversations and collaborations with diverse partners, building on others' ideas and expressing their own clearly and persuasively.

CCSS grade band: K–2

CCSS strand: Speaking and Listening

Anchor standard domain: Comprehension and Collaboration

Grade-Level Standard	What Is Our Current Level of Knowledge About This Standard?	How Can We Increase Our Expertise?	How Will We Measure Our Growth?
Kindergarten **SL.K.1:** Participate in collaborative conversations with diverse partners about kindergarten topics and texts with peers and adults in small and larger groups. a. Follow agreed-on rules for discussions (such as listening to others and taking turns speaking about the topics and texts under discussion). b. Continue a conversation through multiple exchanges.			
Grade 1 **SL.1.1:** Participate in collaborative conversations with diverse partners about grade 1 topics and texts with peers and adults in small and larger groups. a. Follow agreed-on rules for discussions (such as listening to others with care, speaking one at a time about the topics and texts under discussion). b. Build on others' talk in conversations by responding to the comments of others through multiple exchanges. c. Ask questions to clear up any confusion about the topics and texts under discussion.			

Grade 2

SL.2.1: Participate in collaborative conversations with diverse partners about grade 2 topics and texts with peers and adults in small and larger groups.

    a. Follow agreed-on rules for discussions (such as gaining the floor in respectful ways, listening to others with care, speaking one at a time about the topics and texts under discussion).

    b. Build on others' talk in conversations by linking their comments to the remarks of others.

    c. Ask for clarification and further explanation as needed about the topics and texts under discussion.

Source: Adapted from NGA & CCSSO, 2010a, pp. 21–22.

Figure 4.1: Guiding questions for grade-by-grade analysis of the Speaking and Listening standards.

Visit **go.solution-tree.com/commoncore** for a reproducible version of this figure.

Language anchor standard four (L.CCR.4): Apply knowledge of language to understand how language functions in different contexts, to make effective choices for meaning or style, and to comprehend when reading or listening.

CCSS grade band: Grades K–2

CCSS strand: Language

Anchor standard domain: Vocabulary Acquisition and Use

Grade-Level Standard	What Is Our Current Level of Knowledge About This Standard?	How Can We Increase Our Expertise?	How Will We Measure Our Growth?
Grade K			
L.K.4: Determine or clarify the meaning of unknown and multiple-meaning words and phrases based on kindergarten reading and content.			
a. Identify new meanings for familiar words and apply them accurately (such as knowing a *duck* is a bird and learning the verb *to duck*).			
b. Use the most frequently occurring inflections and affixes (such as *-ed, -s, re-, un-, pre-, -ful,* and *-less*) as a clue to the meaning of an unknown word.			
Grade 1			
L.1.4: Determine or clarify the meaning of unknown and multiple-meaning words and phrases based on grade 1 reading and content, choosing flexibly from an array of strategies.			
a. Use sentence-level context as a clue to the meaning of a word or phrase.			
b. Use frequently occurring affixes as a clue to the meaning of a word.			
c. Identify frequently occurring root words (such as *look*) and their inflectional forms (such as *looks, looked,* and *looking*).			

Grade 2

L.2.4: Determine or clarify the meaning of unknown and multiple-meaning words and phrases based on grade 2 reading and content, choosing flexibly from an array of strategies.

a. Use sentence-level context as a clue to the meaning of a word or phrase.

b. Determine the meaning of the new word formed when a known prefix is added to a known word (like happy/unhappy and tell/retell).

c. Use a known root word as a clue to the meaning of an unknown word with the same root (such as *addition* and *additional*).

d. Use knowledge of the meaning of individual words to predict the meaning of compound words (such as *birdhouse, lighthouse,* and *housefly; bookshelf, notebook,* and *bookmark*).

e. Use glossaries and beginning dictionaries, both print and digital, to determine or clarify the meaning of words and phrases.

Source: Adapted from NGA & CCSSO, 2010a, p. 29.

Figure 4.2: Guiding questions for grade-by-grade analysis of the Language standards.

Visit **go.solution-tree.com/commoncore** for a reproducible version of this figure.

of others into the discussion, asking questions, using evidence and examples, and even disagreeing with one another (Michaels, O'Connor, & Resnick, 2008). Anchor standard two (SL.CCR.2) bridges the other two standards by specifying the role that content knowledge plays in these conversations.

1. Prepare for and participate effectively in a range of conversations and collaborations with diverse partners, building on others' ideas and expressing their own clearly and persuasively. (SL.CCR.1)

2. Integrate and evaluate information presented in diverse media and formats, including visually, quantitatively, and orally. (SL.CCR.2)

3. Evaluate a speaker's point of view, reasoning, and use of evidence and rhetoric. (SL.CCR.3) (NGA & CCSSO, 2010a, p. 22)

Presentation of Knowledge and Ideas

The second domain of anchor standards for the Speaking and Listening strand profiles the essential nature of presenting information to one another in more formal ways. Anchor standard four (SL.CCR.4) discusses the ways a speaker organizes and presents information, always keeping the audience and the purpose for the presentation in mind. Anchor standard six (SL.CCR.6) is a reminder that presenters are also listeners and consumers of information. As such, they need to use critical-thinking skills in order to make judgments about the information being shared. Anchor standard five (SL.CCR.5) serves to bridge these two ideas, and it focuses on the presenter's skills in using digital media and visual displays of information, as well as the listener's ability to understand it.

4. Present information, findings, and supporting evidence such that listeners can follow the line of reasoning and the organization, development, and style are appropriate to task, purpose, and audience. (SL.CCR.4)

5. Make strategic use of digital media and visual displays of data to express information and enhance understanding of presentations. (SL.CCR.5)

6. Adapt speech to a variety of contexts and communicative tasks, demonstrating command of formal English when indicated or appropriate. (SL.CCR.6) (NGA & CCSSO, 2010a, p. 22)

Taken together, the anchor standards for Speaking and Listening highlight the integral role of peers in the learning process. Long gone is the notion that all knowledge emanates from the teacher and that the student's chief role is to listen quietly and take it all in (Frey et al., 2009). Peer learning has become a dominant feature in 21st century classrooms, which carries implications for how teachers enable students to interact. These standards are not about being able to pass on pleasantries to one another; they are the engine of learning. Before we examine the specific Speaking and Listening standards for grades K–2, we consider what is known about peer learning.

The Power of Peer Learning

Perhaps the most influential theorist on the role of peer-assisted learning is Lev Vygotsky (1978), who states that all learning is the product of sociocultural phenomena mediated by interactions with others. These social interactions shape the learner's view of the world. Therefore, collaboration with peers becomes a necessary part of the learning process of a child. Indeed, Vygotsky identifies both the teacher and peers as important agents in the learning process (Crain, 2000).

One of Vygotsky's most enduring contributions to education is the concept of a *zone of proximal development*, which describes tasks a learner can successfully complete with minimal assistance. Students who assist one another in completing a task that might otherwise be too difficult for either to complete alone are considered to be working within their zone of proximal development. Many of us have found ourselves working in a group in which the problem is solved through discussion. This is why collaborative planning teams are so powerful: we all enjoy learning and producing in the presence of our peers. So it is with peer learning.

In addition to solving the task at hand, another goal of this type of learning is to foster mastery of skills and strategies that can be used independently in the future. This learning occurs when these "external and social activities are gradually internalized by the child . . . creat[ing] internal dialogues that form the processes of mental regulation" (Wood, 1998, p. 98). Stated differently, the language two students use to figure out a task together eventually becomes part of the internal problem-solving processes each child uses independently.

The power of peer-to-peer learning has been well documented in the research base on effective instruction, and it lies at the heart of all academic discussions (Mueller & Fleming, 2001; Stevens & Slavin, 1995). When students work collaboratively on a task, they are able to clarify one another's understandings, explore possible solutions, analyze concepts, and create new products (Frey, Fisher, & Everlove, 2009). Additionally, they provide an ideal arena for the teacher to observe learning as it takes place, especially through listening to the problem-solving strategies that students use as they wrestle with concepts, skills, and ideas. The anchor standards articulate a path for students to regularly engage in these kinds of collaborative learning processes so that students can construct—not just assimilate—knowledge and share it with others. In the next section, we will examine how peer learning forms the basis for the Speaking and Listening standards for grades K–2.

Speaking and Listening Standards for Grades K–2

The six grade-level standards for Speaking and Listening are organized in the same manner as the anchor standards they are derived from: Comprehension and Collaboration and Presentation of Knowledge and Ideas. Using the protocol in figures 4.1 and 4.2 (pages 94–97), consider the following questions in your collaborative team.

- What is our current level of knowledge about this standard?

- How can we increase our expertise?

- How will we measure our growth?

Alternatively, you and your team may prefer to use the analysis questions from chapters 2 and 3 (pages 23 and 61). Whichever set of questions you select to guide your discussions, you will be working within a framework that enables you to better understand and implement the CCSS.

Comprehension and Collaboration

The three anchor standards in this domain describe the dispositions and purposes of informal talk in the classroom (see table 4.1). Throughout K–2, students are expected to be prepared to participate in discussions with peers, especially as it applies to the norms of discussion. For example, the students in Ms. Martinez-Garza's mathematics class are expected to link their comments to others in order to develop ideas. This expectation is another example of the interplay between the ELA and mathematics standards: Mathematical Practice 3, Construct viable arguments and critique the reasoning of others, involves students in sharing their ideas and responding to each other (NGA & CCSSO, 2010e, pp. 6–7).

Another notable feature of this domain is that its standards are intertwined with other domains of the Common Core ELA standards. For example, collaborative reading experiences provide students with opportunities to make meaning of a text with their peers. When students read and discuss texts together, they apply comprehension strategies and support the understanding of others. We use *collaborative reading* as an umbrella term to describe a number of peer-reading activities, including partner reading and echo reading. Descriptions of these activities, which follow table 4.1, will help you understand the interrelated nature of the ELA standards across kindergarten and grades 1 and 2.

Partner Reading

Partner reading is well-suited for younger students and those who have had little experience with peer learning. Students work in pairs to read and discuss a common text together. When working in partners, students may ask each other questions, make predictions, or clear up confusions.

For example, after participating in a focus lesson on tracking two characters' dialogue using markers like *he said* and *she replied*, first-grade students Brittany and Adriana work together to identify which character is speaking in a passage from the book *Junie B. Jones and the Stupid Smelly Bus* (Park, 1992). They first use two different highlighters to distinguish the speech of each character, then read it aloud together by assuming the role of one of the characters. Next, they switch roles and read to one another again.

Partner reading improves reading fluency through repeated reading. A challenge to building fluency is that it is most effectively accomplished through repeated readings of the same passage. However, this may not be perceived as motivating and interesting to many students, especially those who protest, "I already read that part!" Partner reading can provide the necessary purpose when the task is structured to give students a reason to read more than once because they have someone to read to and with.

Table 4.1: Speaking and Listening Standards for Domain Comprehension and Collaboration, Grades K–2

Anchor Standards	Kindergarten Standards	Grade 1 Standards	Grade 2 Standards
SL.CCR.1: Prepare for and participate effectively in a range of conversations and collaborations with diverse partners, building on others' ideas and expressing their own clearly and persuasively.	**SL.K.1:** Participate in collaborative conversations with diverse partners about kindergarten topics and texts with peers and adults in small and larger groups. a. Follow agreed-on rules for discussions (such as listening to others and taking turns speaking about the topics and texts under discussion). b. Continue a conversation through multiple exchanges.	**SL.1.1:** Participate in collaborative conversations with diverse partners about grade 1 topics and texts with peers and adults in small and larger groups. a. Follow agreed-on rules for discussions (such as listening to others with care, speaking one at a time about the topics and texts under discussion). b. Build on others' talk in conversations by responding to the comments of others through multiple exchanges. c. Ask questions to clear up any confusion about the topics and texts under discussion.	**SL.2.1:** Participate in collaborative conversations with diverse partners about grade 2 topics and texts with peers and adults in small and larger groups. a. Follow agreed-on rules for discussions (such as gaining the floor in respectful ways, listening to others with care, speaking one at a time about the topics and texts under discussion). b. Build on others' talk in conversations by linking their comments to the remarks of others. c. Ask for clarification and further explanation as needed about the topics and texts under discussion.
SL.CCR.2: Integrate and evaluate information presented in diverse media and formats including visually, quantitatively, and orally.	**SL.K.2:** Confirm understanding of a text read aloud or information presented orally or through other media by asking and answering questions about key details and requesting clarification if something is not understood.	**SL.1.2:** Ask and answer questions about key details in a text read aloud or information presented orally or through other media.	**SL.2.2:** Recount or describe key ideas or details from a text read aloud or information presented orally or through other media.
SL.CCR.3: Evaluate a speaker's point of view, reasoning, and use of evidence and rhetoric.	**SL.K.3:** Ask and answer questions in order to seek help, get information, or clarify something that is not understood.	**SL.1.3:** Ask and answer questions about what a speaker says in order to gather additional information or clarify something that is not understood.	**SL.2.3:** Ask and answer questions about what a speaker says in order to clarify comprehension, gather additional information, or deepen understanding of a topic or issue.

Source: Adapted from NGA & CCSSO, 2010a, pp. 22–23.

The transactions between students doing partner reading can take a turn for the worse if not closely monitored and supported. Laurie MacGillivray and Shirl Hawes (1994) conducted a study of the negotiated roles of students during partner reading. They identify the following four possible role sets.

1. **Coworkers:** Children share the workload equally and assist each other.

2. **Fellow artists:** Students perform for each other.

3. **Teacher and student:** One child models and instructs while the other follows.

4. **Boss and employee:** One child does all the work while the other supervises.

In particular, the last role set is clearly not productive. Students benefit from guidelines for effective partner reading, notably those that create ways for them to self-assess. These guidelines include the following.

- Taking turns and listening to one another as they read

- Helping one another when encountering a difficult word

- Making encouraging and positive statements

- Waiting for each other before beginning a new passage

Partner reading is a relatively easy instructional arrangement to implement and is particularly suitable for use at the beginning of the school year, for younger or less experienced students, and when the focus of the task is on practice.

Echo Reading

Echo reading is a related partner reading activity in which students again work in pairs. One student first reads a paragraph aloud then the other repeats the paragraph. Poetry and picture books with rhyming sentences are particularly suitable for echo reading because the students can experience the rhythms and cadence of lively prose. Kindergarteners enjoy echo reading books like *Five Little Monkeys Jumping on the Bed* and its familiar refrain "then the doctor said, 'No more monkeys jumping on the bed!'" (Christelow, 1989). Second graders can practice poems for two voices, such as "Fireflies" (Fleischman, 2004).

Presentation of Knowledge and Ideas

Anchor standards four through six of this domain mirror those in the preceding domain. While the first three standards emphasize informal talk, these address skill development for the more formal talk of presentations that becomes prominent in third grade. Additionally, the standards describe the necessary skills the speaker should exhibit (see table 4.2, page 103). Efficient presentation skills, whether face-to-face or in a digital environment, require the speaker to follow these constructs.

- Organize the information into a logical sequence so that listeners and viewers can comprehend it.

- Have deep and accurate subject knowledge of the topic.

Table 4.2: Speaking and Listening Standards for Domain Presentation of Knowledge and Ideas, Grades K–2

Anchor Standards	Kindergarten Standards	Grade 1 Standards	Grade 2 Standards
SL.CCR.4: Present information, findings, and supporting evidence such that listeners can follow the line of reasoning and the organization, development, and style are appropriate to task, purpose, and audience.	**SL.K.4:** Describe familiar people, places, things, and events and, with prompting and support, provide additional detail.	**SL.1.4:** Describe people, places, things, and events with relevant details, expressing ideas and feelings clearly.	**SL.2.4:** Tell a story or recount an experience with appropriate facts and relevant, descriptive details, speaking audibly in coherent sentences.
SL.CCR.5: Make strategic use of digital media and visual displays of data to express information and enhance understanding of presentations.	**SL.K.5:** Add drawings or other visual displays to descriptions as desired to provide additional detail.	**SL.1.5:** Add drawings or other visual displays to descriptions when appropriate to clarify ideas, thoughts, and feelings.	**SL.2.5:** Create audio recordings of stories or poems; add drawings or other visual displays to stories or recounts of experiences when appropriate to clarify ideas, thoughts, and feelings.
SL.CCR.6: Adapt speech to a variety of contexts and communicative tasks, demonstrating command of formal English when indicated or appropriate.	**SL.K.6:** Speak audibly and express thoughts, feelings, and ideas clearly.	**SL.1.6:** Produce complete sentences when appropriate to task and situation. (See grade 1 Language standards one and three for specific expectations.)	**SL.2.6:** Produce complete sentences when appropriate to task and situation in order to provide requested detail or clarification. (See grade 2 Language standards one and three for specific expectations.)

Source: Adapted from NGA & CCSSO, 2010a, pp. 22–23.

- Ensure graphically displayed information is coherent, accurate, well designed, grammatically correct, and free of misspellings.

- Deliver the information smoothly, and give attention to the audience's needs (for example, eye contact, elocution, and so on).

In the primary grades, students are learning to organize their thoughts in logical ways that enable them to begin to acknowledge the needs of the listener. In kindergarten and first grade, these skills are accomplished primarily through face-to-face interactions, as well as in writing. In second grade, these expand further to audio recordings. You may recall from chapter 3 on writing that first-grade teacher Ms. Elliot records her students' original poems on VoiceThread (www.voicethread.com), a digital storytelling website that allows viewers to record their own questions and comments. Her second-grade colleague Ed Lin builds on these skills. "We're studying fossils in science and reading informational texts such as *Fossils Tell of Long Ago* [Aliki, 1990] and *Digging Up Dinosaurs* [Aliki, 1988]," he says. "We're taking photographs of our science work, and students are making illustrations and diagrams of things like trilobites and the tools archaeologists use. We even took pictures of the dinosaur displays on our field trip to the natural history museum." Mr. Lin scanned all of these photos, and students are using the pictures to assemble a digital story containing three images, as well as recording their original scripts. "These productions are very simple at this point, but I want the students to experience sharing information with others in an organized way," Mr. Lin says. "Because they get to hear what other viewers are thinking about, their sense of audience is strengthened."

Grades K–2 students are not experienced in the demands of formal presentations, and are likely to need considerable support in sharing their knowledge with others in formal ways. It's helpful to tie these formal presentations to the writing standards, as presentations are usually written before they are delivered. Given that there is a parallel emphasis on organization in the writing standards, students should be encouraged to convert these written products into formal presentations. The *paragraph frame* is a useful instructional scaffold for doing both. It is a series of sentence stems intended to scaffold original writing while furnishing an organizational structure. Paragraph frames are not intended as fill-in-the-blank exercises. Instead, they should be introduced after rich oral development of ideas and concepts. This preliminary stage of oral composition assists writers in organizing their own thoughts about a topic as they engage in informal talk (see standards one to three in table 4.1, page 101). The paragraph frame is introduced, and students are instructed to add original sentences within or after it. This procedure is more sophisticated than traditional story starters, which begin with a sentence stem, like "It was a dark and stormy night," because it provides more structure for the writer. A paragraph frame might look like this:

"My favorite book is _____ by _____ . The kind of person who would like this book is _____ . One reason I like this book is because _____ _____ . Another reason is because _____ . If you are the kind of person who likes _____ and _____ , you will enjoy _____ !"

Notice that the frame establishes a direction for the writer without being prescriptive. Furthermore, the writers do not need to use these sentences in sequence but can add their own original writing within the frame. As noted previously, writers can also add to or extend the topic further. These frames can be easily created to reflect informational writing as well. For example:

"Plants are living things. A native plant that lives in our area is _____ . This plant needs lots of _____ to survive. But if it gets too much _____ _____ , it might die. This plant lives for _____ , and it scatters its seed by _____ . You can see a _____ at _____ ."

Once written, these paragraph frames organize informal presentations as well, especially in sequencing facts, events, or concepts in a logical order. Other sample paragraph frames appear in figure 4.3.

Narrative
I'm going to tell you a story about a _____ and a _____. The first _____ said to the second _____, "I wonder _____." The second _____ replied, "I think _____." The two _____ worked together and solved the problem!
Biographical and Autobiographical
On my first day of school in kindergarten, I _____. But then I met _____. Now I know that _____!
Informational and Explanatory
When there is an emergency, you can count on _____ to help. But you have to help by calling them! First, you dial 911. The next step is _____. Don't forget to _____! Finally, remember to _____. If you do all these things, you will make it easy for _____ to help you.

Figure 4.3: Sample paragraph frames for writing and formal presentations.

Anchor standard six (SL.CCR.6) for Speaking and Listening in first and second grades specifically references Language anchor standard one (L.CCR.1) on using the conventions of English in speech and in writing. In terms of the speaking portion of the standard this means using the correct grammar and syntax of conventional English. This can be challenging for students learning English or for some students with language disabilities that make learning English difficult. These students might require more support.

First-grade teacher Jane Caldwell uses simple language frames to support her students who require oral language development. These language frames work similarly to paragraph frames but are developed to support conversational exchanges. In the first week of school, Ms. Caldwell introduces partner talk using language frames to scaffold the students' conversations, about favorite food, books, subjects, and colors. Visit www .youtube.com/user/FisherandFrey for examples of introducing language frames and partner talk to first-grade students. In this video, you will see how to bring the standards in the domains Comprehension and Collaboration and Presentation of Knowledge and Ideas to life in the classroom.

Anchor Standards for Language

A final set of Common Core ELA standards is dedicated to language. Speech and language are closely related, but they do have distinct features that make them unique. Speech concerns verbal expression; language describes what words mean (vocabulary), how they are strung together to make sense using the rules of the language (grammar and syntax), how new words are made (conjugation), and what word combinations work best for a specific situation (pragmatics and register) (American Speech-Language-Hearing Association, 2012). Language is foundational to what we do—it's integral to our behavior. Consequently, it can be difficult to distance ourselves from it in order to observe it. As the saying goes, "The last thing a fish notices is the water it swims in." Language is to humans as water is to fish. By the way, your ability to understand that last idiom and its analogy speaks to your command of language. The NGA and CCSSO (2010a) put it a different way:

> The inclusion of Language standards in their own strand should not be taken as an indication that skills related to conventions, effective language use, and vocabulary are unimportant to reading, writing, speaking, and listening; indeed, they are inseparable from such contexts. (p. 25)

The overall intent of the Language standards speaks to the need to raise our students' awareness of language, something they are not likely to be able to do without an aware teacher's intentional instruction. As a reminder, you may want to analyze the standards for the grades K–2 band with these questions in mind: (1) What is our current level of knowledge about this standard? (2) How can we increase our expertise? and (3) How will we measure our growth?

In the next section, we will examine the anchor standards for Language, which are foundational to the grade-level standards. The anchor standards are organized in three domains: (1) Conventions of Standard English, (2) Knowledge of Language, and (3) Vocabulary Acquisition and Use.

Conventions of Standard English

The two anchor standards in this domain focus on the grammatical rules of spoken and written language, especially as they pertain to parts of speech, written conventions, and spelling. These are essential to communication, and involve issues related to the development of complex sentences, as well as voice and mood.

1. Demonstrate command of the conventions of standard English grammar and usage when writing or speaking. (L.CCR.1)

2. Demonstrate command of the conventions of standard English capitalization, punctuation, and spelling when writing. (L.CCR.2) (NGA & CCSSO, 2010a, p. 25)

Knowledge of Language

This domain has a single anchor standard that covers quite a bit of territory. Beginning in grade 2 (the standard doesn't apply to kindergarten or first grade), students begin to attend to the registers of language, especially in comparing formal and informal modes. By high school, students are applying their knowledge of language through the use of style guides like the Modern Language Association (MLA) style. This anchor standard is strongly linked to others in Writing (for example, W.CCR.4) and Speaking and Listening (for example, SL.CCR.4).

3. Apply knowledge of language to understand how language functions in different contexts, to make effective choices for meaning or style, and

to comprehend more fully when reading or listening. (L.CCR.3) (NGA & CCSSO, 2010a, p. 25)

Vocabulary Acquisition and Use

This domain has received considerable attention in the educational community because of the emphasis on word solving in anchor standard four (L.CCR.4). While this approach to vocabulary development has been widely researched (see Baumann, Font, Edwards, & Boland, 2005; Blachowitz & Fisher, 2002), in practice there has been a more prominent focus on vocabulary lists. As anchor standard six (L.CCR.6) illustrates, grade-level vocabulary lists are valuable. Every teacher should have a strong sense of the grade-level vocabulary expectations. However, this should be coupled with purposeful instruction on how to solve for unknown words.

A second area of attention has been on nuanced use of language in anchor standard six. Note that it defines vocabulary as "words and phrases," not single words alone. In addition, it describes these words and phrases as *general academic* and *domain-specific*. These terms align with the work of Beck et al. (2002) and their description of tier two words (in the language of CCSS, they are general academic words and phrases like *simplify* and *character traits*) that mature language users use in several contexts. In addition, tier three words are those domain-specific words and phrases that are tied to a discipline, like using *habitat* and *desert biome* in science. Anchor standard five (L.CCR.5) draws attention to the need to appreciate the artistry of words that convey just the right meaning, tone, and mood.

4. Determine or clarify the meaning of unknown and multiple-meaning words and phrases by using context clues, analyzing meaningful word parts, and consulting general and specialized reference materials, as appropriate. (L.CCR.4)

5. Demonstrate understanding of figurative language, word relationships, and nuances in word meanings. (L.CCR.5)

6. Acquire and use accurately a range of general academic and domain-specific words and phrases sufficient for reading, writing, speaking, and listening at the college and career readiness level; demonstrate independence in gathering vocabulary knowledge when encountering an unknown term important to comprehension or expression. (L.CCR.6) (NGA & CCSSO, 2010a, p. 25)

Language Standards for Grades K–2

The anchor standards frame a pathway for language development from kindergarten through twelfth grade, with an eye toward systematically preparing students for the language demands of career and college. In this section, we will analyze the specific standards for grades K–2 in more detail.

The six grade-level standards for Language are organized in the same manner as the domains they are derived from: Conventions of Standard English, Knowledge of

Language, and Vocabulary Acquisition and Use. As noted previously, refer to figures 4.1 and 4.2 (pages 94–97) and consider the following questions in your collaborative team.

- What is our current level of knowledge about this standard?

- How can we increase our expertise?

- How will we measure our growth?

Alternatively, you and your team may prefer to use the analysis questions from chapters 2 and 3 (pages 23 and 61). Whichever set of questions you select to guide your discussions, you will be working within a framework that enables you to better understand and implement the CCSS.

Conventions of Standard English

The grade-level standards for this domain speak to the students' acquisition of the rules of grammar and conventions in their spoken and written communication (see table 4.3). A challenge with teaching grammar, punctuation, and written conventions is that the number of rules can quickly overwhelm most learners. Most grammar instruction today calls for teaching it within the context of authentic reading, writing, and speaking demands (Weaver, 1996). Of course, students should be able to identify basic parts of speech, punctuation, and writing conventions. However, learning fewer but powerful rules deeply is more effective than trying to memorize a bewildering list of rules that are soon forgotten. For example, how many of you know what a correlative conjunction (grade 5) is without looking at examples (such as either/or and neither/nor)? Yet you can all use these correctly. From an instructional standpoint, identify the most important labels and rules for your students to know, and place a stronger emphasis on teaching grammar and conventions in context.

Generative Writing

One way to teach these essential language skills in context is through generative writing instruction. Teacher-directed instruction offers a valuable opportunity to provide carefully designed lessons that lead students through an organized process for writing with clarity and originality. However, this does not mean that writing should be reduced to isolated skills at the expense of purpose, voice, content, and conventions. We know that problems can occur when a student is full of ideas but does not possess the means to get the message down on paper. Likewise, the student who has mastered the conventions but has difficulty with generating ideas is equally at risk. Through generative writing instruction, teachers provide students with strategies for creating cohesive writing while engaged in authentic tasks. Linda Dorn and Carla Soffos (2001) describe a continuum of difficulty when completing generative writing:

- Adding words to a text is easier to do.

- Deleting words from a text is harder to do; deleting lines or phrases is even more difficult.

- Substituting words for other words is still more difficult because it requires writers to know multiple meanings for words.

Table 4.3: Language Standard for Domain Conventions of Standard English, Grades K–2

Anchor Standards	Kindergarten Standards	Grade 1 Standards	Grade 2 Standards
L.CCR.1: Demonstrate command of the conventions of standard English grammar and usage when writing or speaking.	**L.K.1:** Demonstrate command of the conventions of standard English grammar and usage when writing or speaking.	**L.1.1:** Demonstrate command of the conventions of standard English grammar and usage when writing or speaking.	**L.2.1:** Demonstrate command of the conventions of standard English grammar and usage when writing or speaking.
	a. Print many upper- and lowercase letters.	a. Print all upper- and lowercase letters.	a. Use collective nouns (such as *group*).
	b. Use frequently occurring nouns and verbs.	b. Use common, proper, and possessive nouns.	b. Form and use frequently occurring irregular plural nouns (such as *feet, children, teeth, mice,* and *fish*).
	c. Form regular plural nouns orally by adding /s/ or /es/ (for example, *dog* and *dogs; wish* and *wishes*).	c. Use singular and plural nouns with matching verbs in basic sentences (for example, *He hops* or *We hop*.).	c. Use reflexive pronouns (such as *myself* and *ourselves*).
	d. Understand and use question words (interrogatives) (like *who, what, where, when, why,* and *how*).	d. Use personal possessive, and indefinite pronouns (such as *I, me, my; they, them, their; anyone,* and *everything*).	d. Form and use the past tense of frequently occurring irregular verbs (such as *sat, hid,* and *told*).
	e. Use the most frequently occurring prepositions (like *to, from, in, out, on, off, for, of, by,* and *with*).	e. Use verbs to convey a sense of past, present, and future (for example, *Yesterday I walked home. Today I walk home. Tomorrow I will walk home.*).	e. Use adjectives and adverbs, and choose between them depending on what is to be modified.
	f. Produce and expand complete sentences in shared language activities.	f. Use frequently occurring adjectives.	f. Produce, expand, and rearrange simple and compound sentences (for example, *The boy watched the movie. The little boy watched the movie. The action movie was watched by the little boy.*).
		g. Use frequently occurring conjunctions (such as *and, but, or, so,* and *because*).	

continued →

Anchor Standards	Kindergarten Standards	Grade 1 Standards	Grade 2 Standards
		h. Use determiners (such as articles and demonstratives).	
		i. Use frequently occurring prepositions (such as *during*, *beyond*, and *toward*).	
		j. Produce and expand complete simple and compound declarative, interrogative, imperative, and exclamatory sentences in response to prompts.	
L.CCR.2: Demonstrate command of the conventions of standard English capitalization, punctuation, and spelling when writing.	**L.K.2:** Demonstrate command of the conventions of standard English capitalization, punctuation, and spelling when writing.	**L.1.2:** Demonstrate command of the conventions of standard English capitalization, punctuation, and spelling when writing.	**L.2.2:** Demonstrate command of the conventions of standard English capitalization, punctuation, and spelling when writing.
	a. Capitalize the first word in a sentence and the pronoun *I*.	a. Capitalize dates and names of people.	a. Capitalize holidays, product names, and geographic names.
	b. Recognize and name end punctuation.	b. Use end punctuation for sentences.	b. Use commas in greetings and closings of letters.
	c. Write a letter or letters for most consonant and short-vowel sounds (phonemes).	c. Use commas in dates and to separate single words in a series.	c. Use an apostrophe to form contractions and frequently occurring possessives.
	d. Spell simple words phonetically, drawing on knowledge of sound-letter relationships.	d. Use conventional spelling for words with common spelling patterns and for frequently occurring irregular words.	d. Generalize learned spelling patterns when writing words (for example, *cage* to *badge*; *boy* to *boil*).
		e. Spell untaught words phonetically, drawing on phonemic awareness and spelling conventions.	e. Consult reference materials, including beginning dictionaries, as needed to check and correct spellings.

Source: Adapted from NGA & CCSSO, 2010a, pp. 25–26.

- Rearranging sentences and paragraphs is the most difficult skill. (pp. 6–7)

Generative sentences draw the writer's attention to the ways grammar, conventions, and vocabulary work together to convey a message. They are initially brief pieces of text that are systematically expanded under the guidance of the teacher. It is based on Fearn and Farnan's (2001) work with *given word sentences* and can be extended through additional scaffolding. A series of prompts are offered to move students from one idea formulated at the letter or word level to a more fully developed piece of connected text. These prompts are usually paced with a timer to keep the lesson moving and to increase fluency at both the written and creative levels.

A generative sentence session for primary-grade writers might begin at the letter level and specify the position within the word. For example, first-grade students are instructed to write words that begin with the letter *c*. After they have written their words, they share words like *cat, cow, can,* and *cut*. Once they have written a word, they now use it in a sentence. The following are sample sentences using the focus words.

- A *cat* is a good pet.
- I saw a *cow* at the farm.
- My mom said I *can* go outside.
- I *cut* the paper with my scissors.

In a matter of minutes, students have moved from considering letters and spelling to factoring content and grammar in order to create a sentence that meets the criteria of the English language. Notice how the writers of the third and fourth sentences had to figure out whether they would use the noun or verb form of the words *can* and *cut*. Stated another way, in a short time the teacher provides a series of tasks that require the writers to consolidate all their cueing systems to develop an original sentence. It is this consolidation of the visual, structural, and contextual processes that is essential to developing fluent writers.

The activity is not completed until it has been extended to the paragraph level. Students can use the sentence they have created as the topic sentence for a paragraph. Now the challenge is to link a series of ideas together to produce a coherent piece of connected text. In a matter of minutes, students have moved across a continuum of writing skills without ever isolating any of those skills at the expense of meaningful writing.

The number of steps used to get to the paragraph level depends on the developmental level of the writers. Emergent and early writers need letter prompts focused at the beginning and end of words, while transitional writers may not need the letter-level prompt at all. A variation of the generative sentence instructional strategy is to begin at the word level. This is especially effective for content-area learning because the teacher chooses the focus word. For example, students can be given the term *pinecone* to construct into accurate sentences. These sentences then serve as a topic sentence for a more detailed informational paragraph that provides the teacher with information about students' content knowledge as well as writing skills. These same procedures can also be used in interactive writing.

Spelling

Anchor standard two (L.CCR.2) describes writing conventions, such as punctuation, capitalization, and spelling. The process of encoding in writing parallels decoding development as students gain control of their reading. Expressive language (speaking and writing) development will always lag behind that of receptive skill levels (listening and reading). You probably notice this with your own literacy as you struggle to spell a word you rarely write, but fully know the meaning and can read it with no difficulty at all.

Researchers have examined the spelling patterns children use. They have named each stage of spelling development: emergent, letter name, within word pattern, syllable juncture, and derivational constancy (Henderson, 1985; Templeton, Johnson, Bear, & Invernizzi, 2008).

Most students in grades K–2 fall into the emergent, letter name, and within word pattern stages of spelling development, although some more advanced second graders may be in the syllable juncture phase. The seeds of spelling are sown in the emergent phase, where virtually all kindergarten students begin.

Emergent Stage

Students recognize that print conveys a message, but they are not yet reading. They use scribbles, wavy lines, symbols that resemble letters, and random letters, and they often engage in writing-like activities and include drawings as part of their writing. At this stage, there is no correlation between the letter a child writes and the sound it was intended to represent (Bear et al., 2012).

Instruction at the emergent stage focuses on phonemic awareness read-aloud and sound-play activities such as singing, chanting, and rhyming words. In addition, as students develop their awareness of and skills in phonemic awareness, they need instruction in the concept of word (where a word starts and ends) and concepts about print (English is read top to bottom and left to right) (Clay, 2000). By pointing to individual words while reading aloud, the teacher builds students' awareness of the one-to-one correspondence between the spoken and written word. At this stage, children enjoy multiple re-readings of a single text. This repetition allows them to predict the story's plot and memorize the words for their own reading. Late in the emergent stage, students need instruction in letter knowledge and sound-symbol correlations. They begin to memorize the spelling of common words that they hear and use, including their name, *mom*, or *dad*. Teachers often use word sorts based on the first letter of a word (Johnston, Bear, Invernizzi, & Templeton, 2009). (See pages 114–115 for descriptions of sorts.)

Letter Name Stage

Students entering this stage have started to master sound-symbol relationships and the concept of a word. Researchers label this stage based on evidence that students use the names of letters and their emerging understanding of the alphabetic principle to spell (Bear et al., 2012; Read, 1975). This level of understanding often leads to rather unconventional spellings; for example, KSL for *castle* and PLES for *police*.

As you observe students reading aloud at this stage, you will notice that they read slowly. This pace provides the novice readers time to use picture or context clues to help figure out the unfamiliar words (Ganske, 2000). Similarly, as you observe students writing at this stage, you will notice that they are very purposeful in their writing. They often write each letter deliberately and continually sound out the word to identify the next letter.

Instructional activities at this stage include read-alouds and independent reading of predicable texts as well as texts that have repetition, rhyme, rhythm, or any other features that help the new reader anticipate words (Ganske, 2000). Again, teachers focus attention on the speech-to-print connection and provide explicit phonics instruction. Typically, students need instruction on initial and final consonants, initial blends and digraphs, short vowels, and final blends and digraphs. Teachers also provide focus lessons, often through interactive writing, on concepts about print and common spelling patterns as well as word sorts on word families and common spelling patterns.

Within Word Pattern Stage

At this stage, students are consolidating their growing knowledge of how combinations of letters can be used to figure out unknown ones. By now, students have mastered many of the common sight vocabulary words and can spell them correctly. Because of their knowledge of letter sounds and short vowel patterns, students can read increasingly difficult texts including chapter books (Bear et al., 2011). Students are no longer relying on individual sounds to spell words, but rather can chunk words and use familiar word families and patterns to make either correct or close approximations to conventional spelling (Ganske, 2000). In both reading and writing, students perform these tasks more quickly and can, therefore, read longer texts and write longer papers. As budding writers, they are becoming more adept at considering their audience and establishing a purpose for their writing.

The instructional implications at this stage include an increased focus on the word wall, individual spelling dictionaries, and systematic spelling instruction with self-corrected tests. An instructional shift to "what students use but confuse" (Bear et al., 2012, p. 16) is important. Commonly this shift includes the vowel-consonant-silent *e* (VCE) patterns (such as *make* and *drive*), *r*-controlled vowel patterns (such as *girl* and *hurt*), complex consonant patterns (such as *fight* and *knee*), and abstract vowel patterns that are not clearly long or short (such as *plow* and *boil*) (Ganske, 2000). In addition, students need to focus on homophones (such as *dear/deer* and *their/there/they're*), synonyms (such as *bucket/pail* and *present/gift*), and antonyms (such as *high/low* or *empty/full*). These are often taught via games such as the following.

- **Jeopardy:** Students create a question based on the word or idea that is given to them.

- **Word-wall bingo:** Students add words from the word wall to a bingo card, such that they have different locations for different words. The teacher then calls out word meanings and students cover the word to determine who has bingo first.

- **Concentration:** Teachers write words and their meanings on two different cards, and students turn over cards trying to find the match between the word and its meaning.

- **Cloze activities:** A word is removed from a sentence, producing a fill-in-the-blank action.

Again, word sorts are useful as students sort words based on these various characteristics.

Syllable Juncture Stage

Grades K–2 students rarely exhibit the developmental attributes of this stage; however, it is possible that some second graders will be more skillful readers and writers. At this stage, students spell most common words correctly and have a growing oral vocabulary. Literacy has increased in value for them as they explore various topics, genres, and ideas. Content areas such as social studies, art, music, science, physical education, and mathematics provide students with access to new information as well as a challenge to read and write in increasingly complex ways. Students at this stage "write to persuade, explain, describe, summarize, and question, using such forms as letters, essays, and various types of response logs to convey their ideas" (Ganske, 2000, p. 17). However, they are now challenged with applying the basic spelling patterns they have learned in the early grades to multisyllabic words they are using in their speech and writing. They still rely on letter sounds and patterns within words, not always to good effect (for example, *confushun* instead of *confusion*). In fact, they are spelling syllable by syllable and facing the question of whether or not to double a consonant (for example, *coton* instead of *cotton*). In addition, they are using more compound words that don't require any doubling. Finally, they are learning how the inflection shifts when a new syllable is introduced (for example, *occur* instead of *reoccur*).

The instructional implications for students at this stage focus on words in which the *-ed* or *-ing* ending requires an *e* to be dropped and the final consonant to be doubled (such as *tapped*, *tapping*, and *taping*), doubling the consonant at the syllable juncture (such as *shopping* or *cattle*), and on words with stressed and unstressed syllables (such as *trample* and *hockey*). This is accomplished with teachers' specific instruction on affixes, roots, and bases using sorts (Johnston, Invernizzi, Bear, & Templeton, 2008).

Sorts typically feature words or pictures on individual cards. Students use a mat to keep cards organized. There are two kinds of sort cards.

1. **Sound sorts:** These cards build phonemic awareness and feature pictures of common objects possessing the same initial, medial, or final sounds. For example, cards containing pictures of a sun, pan, panda, saw, and pig can be sorted into words that begin with the sound of /s/ and those that begin with the sound of /p/.

2. **Word sorts:** These cards feature printed words instead of pictures.

Students then organize these cards using one of three conditions.

1. **Closed sorts:** Students organize the cards based on stated categories.

2. **Open sorts:** Students examine all the cards to construct their own categories.

3. **Conceptual sorts:** Students categorize cards based on meaning rather than word structure.

Derivational Constancy Stage

This final stage of spelling development typically begins in middle school and continues through adulthood, but the basis for this eventual stage is formed in the intermediate grades. Students at this stage rarely spell the majority of words incorrectly, and they are beginning to learn that words with similar meanings share common spelling patterns (such as *demonstrate*, *demonstration*, and *demonstrable*). Students at this stage learn about this history of the language as well as the etymology (word origins).

The instructional implications for students at this stage allow the teacher to teach students to scrutinize words for their histories. Importantly, the teacher will often learn a lot about words as his or her students engage in this level of word study. Students should be encouraged to keep word journals and to capture the related etymology for the words in these journals. Often students like to record the first known use of the word, related words, and a typical sentence in which the word is used. As Bear et al. (2011) suggest, the teacher can initiate the word study with a simple question, "Did you find any interesting words in your reading?" (p. 20). In addition, Ganske (2000) suggests that teachers focus on silent and sounded consonants (such as *hasten* and *haste*), affixes, and vowel changes (such as *democracy* to *democratic*).

Knowledge of Language

This domain does not apply to kindergarten and first grade, as the emphasis of the anchor standard itself is on how language shifts depending on the context. In grade 2, students compare formal and informal uses of the language; for example, noting the differences between the registers of memorized speech, such as the Pledge of Allegiance, the formal written language style used in their textbooks, and the informal conversational exchanges authors use when writing dialogue in a narrative text. Table 4.4 (page 116) presents the standards in this domain.

Students learn written language by building words into sentences that represent ideas. They also learn to write through taking away what is not necessary. This taking-away process is critical for good editing. A hallmark of effective writing is the way sentences *hang together* to support the reader's understanding of the message the writer is attempting to convey. An effective technique for teaching about the nuances involved in transforming adequate sentences into those that resonate is sentence combining.

Sentence combining provides students with an opportunity to utilize syntactic knowledge to create more sophisticated sentences. In a typical activity, students work with a

Table 4.4: Language Standards for Domain Knowledge of Language, Grades K–2

Anchor Standard	Kindergarten Standard	Grade 1 Standard	Grade 2 Standard
L.CCR.3: Apply knowledge of language to understand how language functions in different contexts, to make effective use of choices for meaning or style, and to comprehend more fully when reading or listening.	n/a	n/a	**L.2.3:** Use knowledge of language and its conventions when writing, speaking, reading, or listening. a. Compare formal and informal uses of English.

Source: Adapted from NGA & CCSSO, 2010a, pp. 25–26.

passage of syntactically correct but choppy sentences and rework them to create sentences that preserve the original meaning while increasing the flow of the language.

For example, second-grade teacher Marla O'Campo writes sentences for her students to then combine. In one lesson, Ms. O'Campo writes nine sentences about their recent visit to the Museum of Man. She distributes copies of the sentences along with scissors for each of the students to cut apart the sentences. She then challenges them to rewrite the text so that it contains no more than five sentences. Together they perform *sentence surgery*, cutting unnecessary words out of the disjointed statements. Using the sentence strips as manipulatives, the students move them around on the table until satisfied that they have created a smoother sounding document.

Jaban wrote the new passage using strategies of sentence combining. His passage contains six sentences.

> On Tuesday, the most amazing class of second graders visited the Museum of Man. We were most impressed with the Native American area because it described daily life 100 years ago. We enjoyed meeting different people from different tribes. They all told us interesting stories about their ancestors. However, the best part of the day was eating a hand-made tortilla.

It is important to keep in mind what sentence combining can and cannot do. The effectiveness of sentence combining is diminished in the absence of other components of writing instruction. However, like spoken language, a complex weaving of skills must take place in order to result in a meaningful written message. Syntax is an important part of the fabric of language, and these syntactic lessons should be used as one part of a balanced writing program.

Vocabulary Acquisition and Use

The three remaining Language standards are in the domain Vocabulary Acquisition and Use (see table 4.5, pages 118–119). The vocabulary demands on children skyrocket during the school years, and by the end of second grade, students should know the meaning of 6,000 root words (Biemiller, 2005). There is a snowball effect for students with limited vocabulary, especially as they progress in elementary school. In fact, low vocabulary is thought to be a major contributor to the *fourth-grade slump* (Chall & Jacobs, 2003; Scarborough, 2001), which suggests that student achievement stagnates starting in fourth grade. The difference in word knowledge is problematic because of its impact on content learning and reading comprehension.

The fact is that no one could directly teach 6,000 root words, nor would it be effective. Fortunately, students acquire many words and phrases through wide reading and experiences. In addition, they need to know how to resolve unknown words outside the company of an adult. Anchor standard four (L.CCR.4) emphasizes teaching students a problem-solving approach using structural and contextual analysis, as well as resources. We refer to this as looking inside a word (structure) and outside a word (context and resources) (Frey & Fisher, 2009).

Looking Inside a Word: Structure

Students use analysis of structural components such as prefixes, suffixes, and root and base words to figure out unfamiliar words that contain familiar morphemes. When students understand common prefixes like *re-*, *dis-*, and *un-*, as well as suffixes such as *-s/-es*, *-ing*, and *-er/-or*, they can use this knowledge when they encounter a new word. Word roots are also helpful in understanding the meaning of a new word. For instance, when a student is able to recognize the root in the word *port*, he or she can make a good prediction about related words such as *transport* and *portable*.

Looking Outside a Word: Context

Context clues are the signals authors use to explain a word meaning. There are several types of contextual clues readers use to understand a word, including definitions, synonyms, antonyms, and examples. In the following list, the vocabulary word is underlined and the contextual clue is italicized.

- **Definition:** <u>Deciduous</u> trees grow throughout North America. Deciduous trees *lose their leaves each autumn.*
- **Synonym:** The star *twinkled* and <u>glimmered</u> in the night sky.
- **Antonym:** Cinderella was *kind* to people and animals, unlike her <u>cruel</u> stepsisters.
- **Example:** Percussion <u>instruments</u> make a *sound when they are struck.* <u>Drums</u> and <u>bongos</u> are types of <u>percussion</u> instruments.

Looking Outside a Word: Resources

Another way that students figure out unfamiliar words is by using a resource. We don't encourage students to turn to the dictionary first, because we want them to practice their

Table 4.5: Language Standards for Domain Vocabulary Acquisition and Use, Grades K–2

Anchor Standards	Kindergarten Standards	Grade 1 Standards	Grade 2 Standards
L.CCR.4: Determine or clarify the meaning of unknown and multiple-meaning words and phrases by using context clues, analyzing meaningful word parts, and consulting general and specialized reference materials, as appropriate.	**L.K.4:** Determine or clarify the meaning of unknown and multiple-meaning words and phrases based on kindergarten reading and content. a. Identify new meanings for familiar words and apply them accurately (such as knowing *duck* is a bird and learning the verb *to duck*). b. Use the most frequently occurring inflections and affixes (such as *-ed*, *-s*, *re-*, *un-*, *pre-*, *-ful*, and *-less*) as a clue to the meaning of an unknown word.	**L.1.4:** Determine or clarify the meaning of unknown and multiple-meaning words and phrases based on grade 1 reading and content, choosing flexibly from an array of strategies. a. Use sentence-level context as a clue to the meaning of a word or phrase. b. Use frequently occurring affixes as a clue to the meaning of a word. c. Identify frequently occurring root words (such as *look*) and their inflectional forms (such as *looks*, *looked*, and *looking*).	**L.2.4:** Determine or clarify the meaning of unknown and multiple-meaning words and phrases based on grade 2 reading and content, choosing flexibly from an array of strategies. a. Use sentence-level context as a clue to the meaning of a word or phrase. b. Determine the meaning of the new word formed when a known prefix is added to a known word (such as *happy* and *unhappy* or *tell* and *retell*). c. Use a known root word as a clue to the meaning of an unknown word with the same root (such as *addition* and *additional*). d. Use knowledge of the meaning of individual words to predict the meaning of compound words (such as *birdhouse*, *lighthouse*, *housefly*, *bookshelf*, *notebook*, and *bookmark*). e. Use glossaries and beginning dictionaries, both print and digital, to determine or clarify the meaning of words and phrases.

	Grades K	Grade 1	Grade 2
L.CCR.5: Demonstrate understanding of figurative language, word relationships, and nuances in meaning.	**L.K.5:** With guidance and support from adults, explore word relationships and nuances in word meanings. a. Sort common objects into categories (such as shapes or foods) to gain a sense of the concepts the categories represent. b. Demonstrate understanding of frequently occurring verbs and adjectives by relating them to their opposites (antonyms). c. Identify real-life connections between words and their use (such as note places at school that are colorful). d. Distinguish shades of meaning among verbs describing the same general action (such as *walk, march, strut,* and *prance*) by acting out the meanings.	**L.1.5:** With guidance and support from adults, demonstrate understanding of word relationships and nuances in word meanings. a. Sort words into categories (such as colors, clothing) to gain a sense of the concepts the categories represent. b. Define words by category and by one or more key attributes (such as a *duck* is a bird that swims; a tiger is a large *cat* with stripes). c. Identify real-life connections between words and their use (such as note places at home that are cozy). d. Distinguish shades of meaning among verbs differing in manner (such as *look, peek, glance, stare, glare,* and *scowl*) and adjectives differing in intensity (such as *large* and *gigantic*) by defining or choosing them or by acting out the meanings.	**L.2.5:** Demonstrate understanding of word relationships and nuances in word meanings. a. Identify real-life connections between words and their use (such as describe foods that are spicy or juicy). b. Distinguish shades of meaning among closely related verbs (such as *toss, throw,* and *hurl*) and closely related adjectives (such as *thin, slender, skinny,* and *scrawny*).
L.CCR.6: Acquire and accurately use a range of general academic and domain-specific words and phrases sufficient for reading, writing, speaking, and listening; demonstrate independence in gathering vocabulary knowledge.	**L.K.6:** Use words and phrases acquired through conversations, reading and being read to, and responding to texts.	**L.1.6:** Use words and phrases acquired through conversations, reading and being read to, and responding to texts, including using frequently occurring conjunctions to signal simple relationships (such as *because*).	**L.2.6:** Use words and phrases acquired through conversations, reading and being read to, and responding to texts, including using adjectives and adverbs to describe (such as *When other kids are happy that makes me happy*).

Source: Adapted from NGA & CCSSO, 2010a, pp. 25 and 27.

word-solving strategies. We do encourage them to use structural and contextual analysis first, because even if they can't entirely figure out the word's meaning using those two strategies, they at least know something about the word by the time they turn to the resource. Glossaries are especially good, because unlike dictionaries they limit the given meaning to the one used in the related text. In addition, we keep developmental dictionaries in the classroom for students to consult, and bookmark online dictionaries. Finally, we stress that asking another peer is also a legitimate resource, which we use frequently ourselves. In second grade, students begin to use outside resources like glossaries to clarify meaning of unknown words.

Anchor standard five (L.CCR.5) in the domain Vocabulary Acquisition and Use for grades K–2 details the importance of grouping and categorizing words to build and extend schema. In kindergarten and first grade, this is primarily accomplished through adult support, using methods such as *preview-predict-confirm*, an instructional routine that causes young readers to consider what they know about the topic of an informational text to be used in a read-aloud (Yopp & Yopp, 2004). The teacher begins by showing students the visual information (photographs and diagrams) that accompanies the reading, and he or she solicits predictions about possible words or phrases students expect to read or hear (preview). After listing these, the students convene in small groups to record additional predictions, then sort and label the words into categories. The collaborative groups share their category labels with the rest of the class, then return to their own set of sorts to identify three words: (1) a word all the other groups will have, (2) a word no other group will have, and (3) a word they find to be very interesting (predict). After discussing the three words from each group within the context of the reading, the teacher reads the text, and the class discusses which predicted words or phrases the author used and which he or she did not (confirm). Figure 4.4 is the word sort a group of first graders developed in advance of reading the book *Meet the Orchestra* (Hayes, 1995).

Words About Instruments	Words About Musicians	Words About Music
drum	conductor	music
violin	musician	fancy
tuba	play	nice
string	practice	pretty

The word we think everyone will have is *music*.

The word we think no one will have is *conductor*.

The word we think is interesting is *tuba*.

Figure 4.4: Sample first-grade word sort on music.

Anchor standard six (L.CCR.6), the final one in the domain Vocabulary Acquisition and Use, references grade-appropriate general academic and domain-specific words, providing examples of words that students acquire through exposure to language in conversation and in texts. In particular, reading and being read to are specifically called out across the three grade levels. Read-alouds are widely accepted as a primary source for teaching about new words, but it would be an impossible task to provide direct instruction for each vocabulary word a student might encounter. In addition, the source words each grade level identifies will vary according to materials used, student need, and the local context. However, it is essential to have a method for selecting the words that *will* be taught. It is not uncommon for teachers to use a more haphazard approach, such as choosing all the *big words* or those that are unusual. However, this is particularly inefficient for ensuring that students are focusing on critical vocabulary. Therefore, we offer these questions for considering vocabulary words to teach.

- **Conceptual value:** Does the word represent an important concept that is needed in order to understand the reading? For example, in order to understand the content of the book *Animal Disguises* (Weber, 2004), *camouflage* is critical. However, *carpet shark* is a label, and only appears once in the book. An important consideration in choosing vocabulary relates to the usefulness of the word. Some words are concepts, while others are labels. Given that students need to acquire a tremendous volume of vocabulary words each year, it seems careless to squander valuable instructional time on words that function only as labels in a particular reading.

- **Repeatability:** Is the word going to be used throughout the school year? Some words are worth teaching because they are useful and will be used often. For instance, it is worth taking the time to instruct students on the meaning of *confer* because it will be used throughout the year as students work in small groups with one another.

- **Transportability:** Some words should be selected because they will appear in many subjects or content areas. Teaching students the word *features* as it appears in *Animal Disguises* (Weber, 2004) is useful because students will also be using this word in science and social studies.

- **Contextual analysis:** If students can use context clues to determine the word meaning then direct instruction is not necessary. In *Animal Disguises,* readers can use context clues to determine both the meaning of *camouflage* and the examples of it in the following sentences (Weber, 2004):

  > Camouflage is the way in which an animal blends in with its surroundings. It can be the animal's body shape or the color of its coat or skin that helps it match its home. Camouflage is used for two reasons—to hunt or to hide from predators. (p. 6)

- **Structural analysis:** Words that contain affixes and Latin or Greek root words students are familiar with can be analyzed through structural analysis. For example, the word *seabed* may not need to be included in the list of vocabulary words if students understand the meaning of the two words that make this compound word.

- **Cognitive load:** While there is debate about the number of vocabulary words that teachers should introduce to students at a given time, most agree that the number should reflect the developmental level of the students and the length of the reading (Baumann, 2009; Graves & Watts-Taffe, 2002; Nagy & Scott, 2000; Padak, Bromley, Rasinski, & Newton, 2012). In a brief reading, two to three words is often sufficient for emergent and early readers, while transitional readers can utilize five or so. Most agree that no more than ten should be introduced at any time.

Teachers must create a balance between students learning words in context and learning words through systematic, explicit instruction. Our experience suggests that students will learn a great number of words from well-chosen texts *and* from a thoughtful selection of words for intentional instruction.

Conventions in Kindergarten

Interactive writing is a form of writing in which the teacher and students collaborate to produce a composition. This writing activity differs from LEA (see pages 87–88) in two ways. The teacher *shares the pen* with the students, allowing students to write the message for all to see (Williams & Lundstrom, 2007). Another important difference is that interactive writing messages are accurate in both spelling and content because the teacher continues to work with students to revise the writing until it is correct. Like LEA, it is often based on a shared experience and written on large chart paper. Carol Lyons and Gay Su Pinnell (2001) describe five key elements of interactive writing instruction.

1. **Planning:** The first step of the interactive writing lesson is to establish a purpose for the text. Whether it is a response to literature ("What was our favorite part of the story?"), directions for growing a flower, or a class letter for back-to-school night, the reason for writing must be clearly recognized. This is accomplished through teacher-led talk that guides students through an initial gathering of ideas. Like LEA, this may come from a shared experience like reading a book, participating in a class science experiment, or planning an upcoming event.

2. **Deciding the precise text:** All writing consists of formulating ideas that are then narrowed to a specific string of words intended to convey those ideas. Therefore, after ideas have been generated it is necessary to begin to refine the message. Andrea McCarrier, Gay Su Pinnell, and Irene Fountas (2000) refer to this as "negotiation . . . through an active discussion and guided planning" (p. 85). A skillful teacher understands that *all* students—not just the more verbal and assertive members of the class—must feel a connection to the message.

   Word choice is also part of the discussion at this point in the lesson. A major goal of interactive writing is to arrive at a jointly composed message that is semantically and syntactically correct. Therefore, anomalies in vocabulary and grammar must be discussed. The goal is not to simply tell students what to do, but to scaffold their understanding through the use of prompts that will enable them to self-correct errors. For example, a teacher might address a grammatical error by asking students to say the correct and incorrect sentence aloud to decide which version sounds better. For example, students might be asked to decide on the better of these two sentences: "There were two cat on the playground this morning" and "There were two cats on the playground this morning." Once the class reaches consensus and says the correct text aloud, students are ready to commit the message to the page.

3. **Seeing how print works:** Grades K–2 students may have difficulty with the layout of the text on the page, in particular the space needed for and between each word. Directionality, both left to right and top to bottom, must be considered as well. Writers who have mastered print conventions are also learning about punctuation, indention, and capitalization. The teacher first leads students in a rehearsal of the agreed-on message so that students can more easily recall the exact wording. They may also count the words to formulate a prediction about how much space they will need. Finally, the rehearsal should also include the pauses and inflections that will indicate the punctuation necessary. Providing young writers with a wooden clothespin is one way to assist young writers with spacing issues. Using this tool reinforces the essential concept that spacing, as well as the letters themselves, carries meaning.

4. **Analyzing words:** In the typical interactive writing lesson, the teacher leads the class in analyzing each word of the message so students can spell it correctly. A sight word may appear on a word wall and can therefore be copied. Other words are decoded as students use their current knowledge of the way letters and sounds work. The key is for the teacher to have an understanding of what the students currently know in order to scaffold instruction. Teachers should provide letter sounds that are unknown to the students to avoid consuming valuable instructional time devoted to concepts that are too difficult. For example, in October, kindergartners are unlikely to know the /ph/ sound in *phone*. Therefore, the teacher should write this portion of the word and invite the students to listen to the final consonant sound. The /n/ phoneme is in their current repertoire, so students should write it.

The teacher leads the students through the process of decoding each word, then invites a student to write the agreed-on letter on a language chart. The teacher may gently prompt the student where to begin writing the letter and provide additional guidance as needed to enable the student to write the correct letter. All the students then repeat the letter until the entire word has been written. As each word is written, the message is to re-read to make sure that the agreed-on text is being composed and to identify the next word. For example, if the class wanted to write the sentence, "Tomorrow we will go to visit the zoo," and students were unsure about the word *tomorrow*, the teacher would work on that word, letter by letter, and when the word was finished the whole class would read the word and then say the rest of the sentence aloud from memory.

As noted earlier, the goal of interactive writing instruction is to create a message that has correct spelling and syntax. Nonetheless, students are likely to make errors. A permanent ink black marker is a necessary tool in interactive writing. Errors should not be erased but can be dealt with in another way. Erasures can be distracting and upsetting to young writers. Instead, one-inch-wide white correction tape can be used to cover the error. The child then writes the letter correctly on top of the tape. In this way, the student deals with the error quickly, and he or she gets another opportunity to practice it correctly and does not disrupt the flow of the message.

5. **Reading and writing connections:** Reading and writing, like speaking and listening, are closely linked as receptive and expressive forms of literacy. Teachers should explicitly introduce types or genres of writing to students. Genres include poetry, lists, stories, and letters. When composing and constructing original text in interactive writing, teachers should be sure to include a variety of writing genres in the lessons. Interactive writing helps students make connections between reading and writing because they learn to read what they have written and compose in response to what they have read. For example, the opening scenario for this chapter was an innovation lesson in which students explored various mathematical groupings to solve a problem. Interactive writing is also useful for students throughout elementary school, who can benefit from the modeling and scaffolding associated with this instructional technique.

Conclusion

The Common Core State Standards for ELA contain several resources that are of value for your collaborative teams to draw on in future activities. Research supports for the ELA standards are located in appendix A of the CCSS (NGA & CCSSO, 2010b). For example, your team may want to further explore the link between the Speaking and Listening skills and teacher read-alouds. You may recall from chapter 2 on the Reading standards that the text exemplars list read-alouds as a distinct category for grades K–2. The section, "Read-Alouds and the Reading-Speaking-Listening Link" in appendix A (NGA & CCSSO, 2010b) can initiate further team analysis in identifying both the books to use and the Speaking and Listening activities to accompany them.

Another possible area for collaborative team exploration might include spelling. The section "Reading Foundational Skills" in appendix A of the Common Core ELA includes information on orthography (see NGA & CCSSO, 2010b, pp. 17–22). Given that students in grades K–2 are learning to apply concepts of orthography to their reading and writing, the primary planning team may determine that this is a robust area of instruction that can move beyond the conventional program of giving students a list of words on Monday and testing them on Friday.

A third possible path for the collaborative team to follow concerns language grammar and conventions, as well as vocabulary. Again, appendix A (NGA & CCSSO, 2010b) proves a useful resource with a discussion of the relationship of the Conventions of Standard English and Vocabulary Acquisition and Use domains to the Reading, Writing, and Speaking and Listening strands. The description further articulates the integrated nature of language teaching and learning. Additionally, the CCSS offer extensive information on vocabulary and the identification of tier one (everyday-speech), tier two (general-academic), and tier three (domain-specific) words and phrases (see NGA & CCSSO, 2010b, pp. 33–35). The collaborative team may decide to identify vocabulary in tiers two and three that will be taught across the grade band using a schoolwide approach to vocabulary development (Frey & Fisher, 2009).

The Speaking and Listening and Language strands are integral to English language arts, both within the strands of reading and writing, and across the disciplines. Never again should we tell students that "spelling doesn't count" when in mathematics instruction, or that communication skills don't need development because now it's time for social studies. These are foundational to how people learn; all learning is language based. Speaking and listening are used most prominently in the classroom, and the quality of discourse in the classroom is directly related to increased achievement. James Britton (1983) says, "Writing floats on a sea of talk" (p. 1), and we fully agree. In fact, we would go one step further: *learning* floats on a sea of talk.

CHAPTER 5

Implementing Formative Assessments to Guide Instruction and Intervention

KEY QUESTIONS

• In our preparations for teaching the lesson, chapter, or unit, to what extent does your collaborative team use the standards and aligned assignments to guide your planning?

• What assessment instruments have you developed collaboratively? Do these instruments accurately reflect the expectations for student achievement that the standards define?

• How do you use your assessment practices to enable students to better understand their learning strengths as well as their needs? In what ways do your assessment activities build students' confidence and motivation?

• To what extent do your schedules provide for timely assessment feedback to students? If changes are needed, how can you go about making them?

• How can you use your assessment data more effectively to modify instruction and help students achieve success?

Craig Woods, who is concerned about the perfor-mance of one of his kindergarten students, uses a variety of assessments to plan his instruction. Over the first few months of the school year, Mr. Woods collects a variety of assessments and continually revises his instruction. Luis Mario is a kindergartner who just turned five years old. During the first couple of weeks of school, he needs help getting his belt on or off when using the restroom. He walks very slowly in line; if there is a gap in line, more often than not it is Luis Mario. When he speaks, it is very softly with the sound of little bits of extra air escaping from the corners of his mouth. His mother notes that he started preschool the previous year, but was removed because he refused to participate or even speak. His mother reports to Mr. Woods, "He would actually turn his entire body away from the teacher and ignore her." Mr. Woods takes extra steps to make sure Luis Mario is involved and connected to the class. Although he is intermittently inter-ested in what's going on in class, he's still somewhat day dreamy.

On the initial assessment, Luis Mario identifies three capital letters and no lowercase letters and only writes three of the four letters in his first name. Curiously enough, he doesn't recognize two letters he is able to write. This seemingly is a trend in Luis Mario's learning. He has pockets of knowledge, but not necessarily all connected. For example, he can make one-to-one correspondence, but doesn't recognize that letters make words.

Mr. Woods is using a number of assessments he and his collaborative team have selected to guide the instructional plans for Luis Mario. These assessments include a district-created screening tool, the CORE assessment (Consortium on Reading Excellence, 1999), and the Yopp-Singer Test of Phonemic Segmentation (Yopp, 1995). Luis Mario shows very poor letter identification on the district-created screening tool that focuses on letter knowledge and letter-sound correspondence. He shows improvement in these areas on the CORE assessment, which Mr. Woods administered after Luis Mario participated in reciting the alphabet daily, focusing on a single letter weekly, and doing a variety of seatwork activities involving classmates' names for about a month. These results show that Luis Mario is ready for more advanced instruction. Mr. Woods, in discussing Luis Mario with his collaborative planning team notes, "I think that the instruction is starting to help. He's doing really well, but I think he needs more from me." Marsha Fields, another kindergarten teacher, says, "I wonder if we could do some cross-class grouping so that we can target more needs and keep pushing our students. I'd be interested in talking with you outside of the meeting to figure out if that would work."

However, on the Yopp-Singer, which Mr. Craig administers in September, Luis Mario identifies a few beginning sounds but seems confused by the task. Stretching out all the sounds is difficult for him, which clearly is an area that requires focused instruction. His score on this test is zero.

On the Concepts About Print test from the *Observation Survey of Early Literacy Achievement* (Clay, 2002), Luis Mario demonstrates good book-handling skill, recognizes one-to-one correspondence, and demonstrates left-to-right movement and return sweep. However, he is unable to distinguish between one letter and two or between letters and words. Based on the assessment data, many observations of Luis Mario during writing activities, and discussions with his collaborative planning team, Mr. Woods decides that he should focus instruction on letter-sound identification and writing. He knows that Luis Mario's writing needs will be addressed during the whole-class interactive writing lessons. Mr. Woods also decides to focus on letter-sound identification during small-group reading instruction. During one of the collaborative planning sessions, Ms. Fields shares a lesson using an alphabet book, *Alphabet City* (Johnson, 1995). Mr. Woods creates several lessons with alphabet books, including *Zoo Flakes ABC* (Howell, 2002) and *A is for "All Aboard!"* (Kluth & Kluth, 2010), which he uses with Luis Mario during individualized time that he has with students during independent reading and writing.

Mr. Woods refers Luis Mario to the RTI team for review. The team's discussion focuses on what has worked and where Luis Mario still needs help. As Sandi Patterson says, "I think that Luis Mario needs more time with instruction. He seems to be responding, but maybe some additional small group time would help." As a result of the conversations with his collaborative planning team and the RTI team, Mr. Woods provides daily supplemental intervention to Luis Mario focused on letter recognition and phonemics awareness. He makes significant progress over the course of eighteen weeks— by December he can name all the letters of the alphabet, and in January he scores 90 percent on the Yopp-Singer Test. Mr. Woods is very pleased to share information about Luis Mario's progress with his collaborative team. The team has talked about this student on several occasions and provides Mr. Woods with ideas about intervention and additional assessments that could be used to measure progress.

A Collaborative Planning Team in Action

Mr. Wood's collaborative planning team makes a commitment to fold ongoing assessment into their instructional practices, beginning the first day of school. Initially, they collect information about each child as an individual in order to establish a baseline for where to begin. These early assessments allow them to group students and get them started with high-quality instruction. Their instructional units are peppered with formative assessments that make it possible for them to gauge student progress toward goals before the unit has ended. Mr. Woods's team uses the key questions at the opening of the chapter (page 127) to shape its assessment plan. Likewise, we encourage you to use these same questions as you identify, design, and analyze the formative and summative assessments you will use in your classrooms.

In the first part of this chapter, we discuss how a formative assessment plan guides instruction. In the latter half of the chapter, we discuss the use of data to guide an RTI plan for students who struggle.

The Role of Assessment and the Common Core State Standards

Why do teachers assess students? Think about this for a minute. Is it because they want to find out what students do not know? Or is it because assessments and testing are part of the official behaviors of teachers? Or maybe it's because teachers don't know where to begin instruction without good assessment information. Diane Lapp, Douglas Fisher, James Flood, and Arturo Cabello (2001) suggest that teachers assess students for at least four reasons, including to:

1. Diagnose individual student needs (for example, assessing developmental status, monitoring and communicating student progress, certifying competency, and determining needs)

2. Inform instruction (for example, evaluating instruction, modifying instructional strategies, and identifying instructional needs)

3. Evaluate programs

4. Provide accountability information

As educators, we make numerous decisions about instruction that matter in very significant ways. We believe that these decisions must be based on the assessment information that we gather throughout the learning cycle. This means the teacher doesn't merely march lockstep through the content of a standards-based curriculum, but rather balances the content with the learner's needs. These needs are identified through ongoing assessment that is linked to subsequent instruction. In this model, assessment and instruction are considered to be recursive because they repeat as students learn new content. In learner-centered classrooms, teachers first assess to establish what children know and do not know, then plan instruction based on this information. Next, they deliver the instruction they have designed and observe how learners respond. Based on these observations, educators reflect on the results and assess again to determine what needs to be taught next. Figure 5.1 represents this concept.

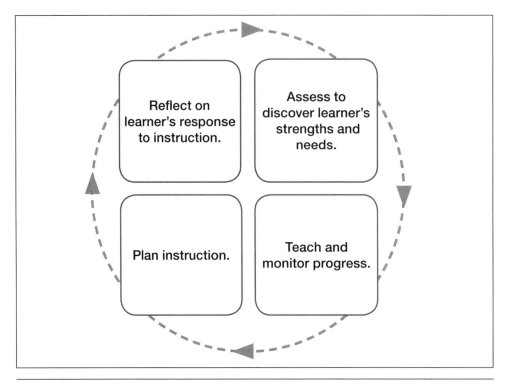

Figure 5.1: Relationship between assessment and instruction.

This model may sound as if it would take a lot of time to complete; in fact, effective teachers perform many of these complex tasks fluidly within the course of their instruction. In well-organized classrooms, assessment happens throughout the day as teachers use questions, discussions, and assignments to measure progress. In addition, teachers administer assessments to monitor progress and formulate future instruction. Assessment equips them with specific information about students who struggle and further informs them about the conditions and content of intervention needed. Teachers are also informed of those students who would benefit from instruction that deepens and enriches their learning. This lies at the very heart of what collaborative planning teams do—they monitor the progress of their students, analyze the results of their teaching, and design intervention supports.

In this chapter, we will concentrate on illustrating assessment events that occur and inform future teaching, so that students can thrive within a Common Core-framed educational system.

Preparing for and responding to large-scale assessments can consume much of the focus and effort of teachers, elementary school principals, and school district administrators, even if those tests are not given in grades K–2. Implementing the CCSS is unlikely to alter the scrutiny and pressure teachers and administrators face from large-scale assessments.

In 2010, the U.S. Department of Education awarded $330 million in Race to the Top funds to two consortia, representing the majority of states, to develop assessments aligned with the CCSS. (See page 11.) SBAC, representing more than thirty states, received $160 million, and PARCC, representing more than twenty-five states, received $176 million. As of this publication, eleven states are members of both consortia (Porter, McMaken, Hwang, & Yang, 2011). Both consortia intend to implement their new state-level common assessments for grades 3–8 and high school during the 2014–2015 school year, which is causing teachers in grades K–2 to focus on the new expectations for demonstrating mastery.

Both assessment consortia aim to design *common* state assessments that are consistent with the vision of the CCSS to include items that assess higher-order thinking, complex texts, writing with evidence, and comparisons across texts. If the assessments take the form their designers intend, then these new state assessments will promote desired instructional changes in favor of an emphasis on deep understanding and reasoning.

Both PARCC and SBAC intend to provide adaptive online tests that will include a mix of constructed-response items, performance-based tasks, and computer-enhanced items that require the application of knowledge and skills. Both assessment consortia are intending to provide summative- and interim-assessment options within the assessment system. You should check your state website for the latest information about progress of the assessment consortia, or visit www.parcconline.org or www.smarterbalanced.org for more information.

For the interim assessments to function as a potential learning tool, teachers will need to ensure they are used for formative purposes—that they are used to provide students and teachers with accurate, timely, fair, and specific information that can move learning forward. This will require that collaborative planning team members are provided time to plan instructional adjustments and that students are supported in relearning content not yet mastered.

However, overreliance on the PARCC and SBAC interim assessments to provide a school district's formative assessment system is not recommended since the effectiveness of this structure to improve student learning is questionable (Popham, 2008). What will make the most difference in terms of student learning is the formative assessment system described later in this chapter. As Wiliam (2007) writes, "If students have left the classroom before teachers have made adjustments to their teaching on the basis of what they have learned about students' achievement, then they are already playing catch-up" (p. 191).

It will be important for team members to become engaged in their state and school's transition to the Smarter or PARCC assessment initiative as part of the full implementation of the Common Core State Standards. The team will need to discuss the following questions.

- How and when will interim assessments be used?

- How will collaborative teams inform families and other members of the school community?

- How will collaborative teams prepare all children in each grade level or school?

Such questions are appropriate as your district- and school-level collaborative teams begin to link state-supported CCSS-related assessments to your implementation of the Common Core State Standards for English language arts. All of this starts with the development and implementation of a formative assessment system. More than formative assessment tools, a *system* allows teachers and teams to systematically evaluate student performance data and make instructional adjustments accordingly. It also allows teams to identify students in significant need and allocate additional support, often through RTI. A formative assessment system that comes from a synthesis of research about the use of student work to inform instruction requires teachers to feed up, feed back, and feed forward.

Feed Up, Back, and Forward

Assessment doesn't begin when the test is passed out; it starts the moment instruction begins. Yet too often assessment is an afterthought, administered mostly to assign a grade. Hattie and Timperley (2007) have an elegant way of describing a model of ongoing assessment: feed up, feed back, and feed forward. We have taken this model a step further to articulate a concrete plan for doing so; one in which we add checking for understanding to the mix (Frey & Fisher, 2011) as a way to feed up by using methods to analyze and assess student understanding. Additionally, we offer a protocol for developing common pacing guides and curricula.

Feed Up by Establishing Purpose

When learners know what is expected of them, what they should be learning, and how they will demonstrate their mastery, their knowledge acquisition is accelerated. This requires clear statements of purpose in order to orient students and make learning intentional. As teachers, we are long accustomed to the practice of defining learning objectives for a lesson: "Students will infer what animals eat from the shapes of their teeth." But how often are these learning targets shared with the people who are supposed to demonstrate them? Establishing purpose means that these intentions are shared with the students and are used as a guideline for the formative assessment that follows.

We advise further identifying your purpose across three dimensions: (1) content, (2) language, and (3) social purpose. Content is usually the easiest, and the one we often think of first when relating it to objectives. It is the discipline-specific knowledge students should acquire *today*. Inferring the diet of an animal based on its teeth is an example of a content purpose for first graders. But how will they demonstrate it? Will they use a graphic organizer to compare and contrast different types of teeth? Will they meet in collaborative groups and describe the characteristics of different teeth using evidence from the text? Will they identify the similarities and differences in a written summary? All of these are related to the language purpose. As we discussed in chapter 4, language is pervasive and includes written and verbal forms, as well as levels of cognition. Finally, a social purpose is useful for students in grades K–1 who are learning to learn collaboratively. A social purpose in this lesson might be to provide evidence and examples to help others understand, or to demonstrate listening comprehension by building on others' comments during a class discussion.

Brenda Jordan uses a feed-up process with every lesson she teaches in her second-grade classroom. "This was a focus of our team for a while. We developed purpose statements to accompany all of our lessons. Most of us write them on the board so that the students can see them, and it's a good reminder to remember to start off the lesson by making sure they know what we'll be doing, and why," she explains. She relays to her collaborative team that initially doing this was a daunting task. "We made the mistake of leaving it up to individual teachers to do, but we quickly realized there was a lot of duplication of effort," she recalls. She also cites their guiding questions, featured at the beginning of this chapter. "That first question, 'In our preparations for teaching the lesson, chapter, or unit, to what extent do we use the standards and aligned assessments to guide our planning?' was crucial for us. Developing purpose statements together led to lots of good discussion about what we were teaching, and for what purposes."

Checking for Understanding

This is an ongoing process of assessment to determine to what extent students understood the lesson and to find out what gaps remain. As such, checking for understanding lies at the heart of formative assessment and is probably the first thing that comes to mind when teachers think about assessment. There are a variety of methods to check for understanding, including using oral language activities, questions, writing, projects and performances, and tests (Fisher & Frey, 2007a).

Oral Language Activities

When students are doing the talking, the teacher has a chance to assess understanding. A number of classroom structures provide students an opportunity to talk, including think-pair-share, reciprocal teaching, literacy circles, discussion prompts, and Socratic seminars. For example, as Ms. Jordan listens to her students discussing a text they are reading as part of their book club, she notices that they are not justifying their responses with evidence from the text. They are skilled at summarizing, but the lack of evidence in their discussions indicates a need to devote additional instructional time to this practice.

In addition to listening as students interact, retellings are a valuable way to check for understanding. Retellings provide the teacher with a glimpse into student thinking. For example, second-grade teacher Mark Kratz asks Ruben to retell a section of a video clip students watched related to rock formation. As part of his retelling, Ruben says, "Sometimes small rocks can be formed because of the weather. That can happen when water runs over the rock for a long time, like in the Grand Canyon. Small rocks can also get formed when bigger rocks break, like we saw in the earthquake part of the video." This retelling lets Mr. Kratz know that much of his teaching has stuck and that Ruben is well on his way to understanding rock formation.

Questions

Questioning, which can be done orally or in writing, is the most common way that teachers check for understanding. Unfortunately, not all questions are worthy of instructional time. To be useful, the initial questions teachers ask should be planned in advance. Of course, additional questions that probe student understanding will come to mind during the interactions teachers have with students, but these initial questions form the expectations for student understanding. Less helpful questions are those we like to call *guess what's in the teacher's head*. More formally known as *initiate-respond-evaluate* or *IRE* (Cazden, 2001), this cycle privileges students who are willing to play the game. For example, Nikola Slobodan asks his second graders, "Can you name one of the simple machines?" Three or four students raise hands, and Martha is selected to respond. Martha says, "Pulley," to which the teacher responds, "Good." IRE is typically used with recall information and provides only a few students an opportunity to respond.

Instead, quality checking for understanding suggests that teachers need to ask questions that require more complex and critical thinking and that lots of students need to respond. A number of instructional routines provide students with practice in questioning habits, such as *reciprocal questioning* or *ReQuest* (Manzo, 1969) in which students read with a partner, taking turns asking and answering questions. As they practice, their teacher analyzes the types of questions being asked and the appropriateness of the answers. Over time (and with instruction and practice) students tire of the literal and recall questions and move toward more interesting questions that require synthesis and evaluation.

Another way to question in an inclusive way is through audience-response systems. These can be as basic as 3 × 5 cards with answers on them that all students hold up to answer a question to as complex as hand-held devices that allow each student to key in a response to a question. As an example of the former, as part of their discussions about *The Raft* (LaMarche, 2000), Ms. Green provides her second-grade students with green and red cards, with *Yes* written on the green card and *No* written on the red card. As she reads each statement about the book, students hold up one of their cards to indicate if they agree or disagree. A question about character traits splits the class, which provides the teacher information about where to focus the lesson next.

Writing

When students are writing, they are thinking. In fact, it's nearly impossible to write and *not* think. That's why short writing-to-learn prompts are so effective for checking for understanding. It's important to develop the prompt so it provides teachers with information about student understanding. For example, the RAFT writing prompt (Santa & Havens, 1995) requires that students consider the role, audience, format, and topic in their writing; this is an excellent way to check for understanding. There are, of course, many other writing prompts that can be used, but RAFT is flexible and teaches perspective. A simple RAFT for first graders might look like this.

R Goldilocks

A The Three Bears

F Letter

T Apology

In order to successfully complete this RAFT, students must understand the story, the characteristics of a letter, and the social language of apologies. This RAFT writing frame works equally well for expository writing.

Projects and Performances

On a larger scale, teachers can use projects and performances to check for understanding. Importantly, this should not be done at the end when the project is completed, but rather as students work on these types of activities. A wide range of appropriate projects and performances allows students an opportunity to engage in meaningful work aligned with content standards. As we have noted in chapter 4, the Speaking and Listening standards require that students present, and this category is important for checking for understanding as students learn to demonstrate mastery of these standards. Useful projects and performances range from presentations to group tasks like creating visual displays.

Tests

Although tests are typically considered a summative assessment tool used for grading and evaluating student performance, they can also be used to check for understanding. Incorrect answers on a test provide teachers with information about what students still need to learn. Tests can be developed in a number of different formats, ranging from multiple-choice to dichotomous choice (like true/false, yes/no, and agree/disagree) to essays.

Developing Common Pacing Guides and Curricula

Many assessments that are used to check for understanding are designed and implemented by the collaborative planning team in order to gather and analyze data. The Common Core State Standards in English language arts will present a new set of challenges for teachers and administrators. Common assessments, consensus scoring, and item analysis will figure prominently in developing new pacing guides and curricula.

You can use the collaborative team meeting record (see figure 1.2, page 18) to do so. The five steps include (Fisher & Frey, 2007a) the following.

1. Construct an initial pacing guide for instruction to frame the team's work. Designed to frame the team's work, this guide should be aligned to the outcome standards stated in the CCSS.

2. Identify instructional materials such as texts, websites, and media for each unit of study in the pacing guide.

3. Develop common formative assessments and a schedule for administering them. These should include formative and summative measures and will provide the team with data to analyze.

4. Engage in consensus scoring and item analysis. These actions serve to determine how students did, and to explore the relationship between teaching and learning. It is useful to disaggregate the data to identify trends within and across significant subpopulations. The intent of this is not to drill down to the individual teacher level, but rather to look across the grade level and grade band to locate patterns. For example, if students with disabilities are making good progress, then what accommodations can this be attributed to? Remember that these data analysis events are also for identifying areas of instructional strength, not just locating areas of need.

5. Make revisions to instruction and curriculum and the formation of intervention groups. The outcomes of these team meetings should have dual purposes. The first is to refine instruction for all students in order to improve acquisition of knowledge. In addition, the team needs to examine the circumstances that might be preventing identified students from making sufficient progress. For some students, this may be a matter of reteaching. For those who are displaying a pattern of difficulties, that may warrant more formal intervention. Later in this chapter, we will discuss RTI as a model for meeting the needs of students who struggle.

Feed Back to Build Student Agency

It would be a mistake to isolate checking for understanding from the feedback loop. Think about the third planning questions for a moment: How do you use your assessment practices to enable students to better understand their learning strengths as well as their needs? In what ways do your assessment activities build students' confidence and motivation? Students need feedback to guide their learning throughout the process. But not all feedback is useful. The evidence on scoring as feedback suggests that when done in isolation from other types of feedback such as feedback about processing of the task, it undermines future achievement (Wiliam, 2011). To make feedback more robust, use it judiciously (Hattie & Timperley, 2007). Consider the following forms of feedback.

- **Feedback about the task** (corrective feedback) is effective for alerting a learner to errors. But it is not effective when the student lacks the skills or the knowledge needed to complete the task.

- **Feedback about the processing used in the task** is highly effective because it reminds the learner about his or her cognitive and metacognitive thinking. For example, "I see you're underlining the parts of the story that are important for telling us about the character. That's keeping your ideas organized."

- **Feedback about self-regulation** is also very effective because it assists the learner in self-assessing. For instance, "You were frustrated earlier when your group wasn't listening to your ideas, but you stayed cool and tried again. Did you notice how they listened when you gave them another chance?"

- **Feedback about the person** is considered ineffective because it doesn't provide the learner with any information about what to do next. For example, "Way to go!"

The fourth planning questions are also related to feedback: To what extent do your schedules provide for timely assessment feedback to students? If changes are needed, how can you go about making them? Even the best feedback will lose its effectiveness if it is not *timely*. In addition, the feedback must be *actionable;* that is, the learner should have a clear sense of direction about what she should do next. Additionally, feedback should be *specific* so that the learner is equipped with a necessary level of detail about his or her next actions. Of course, it should be *understandable*, in the sense that it should be developmentally and cognitively appropriate for the learner. Taken together, feedback that is well thought out and delivered in a timely fashion will build the agency of the learner and encourage him or her to assume more responsibility for his or her own learning. Because the learner *can*. After all, "Feedback should cause thinking" (Wiliam, 2011, p. 127).

Feed Forward to Inform Instruction

The process of formative assessment is incomplete unless it feeds forward into future instruction. The classroom is the unit of analysis, and the purpose is to locate students who need further instruction *during* (not after) the unit of study. This requires some recordkeeping in order to analyze errors students are making. In our efforts to get to know students as individual learners, we can lose track of patterns that are otherwise right in front of us. Call it the phenomenon of not seeing the forest for the trees, if you will. Error analysis allows us to gain a bit of perspective on who is having difficulty and further prevents us from expending so much effort attending to individual learning problems that we run out of time to instruct everyone.

Error analysis can be accomplished in a number of ways, from a commercially prepared checklist to one the teacher makes. This links back to being clear about the purpose, and these purpose statements can be used as a platform for clarifying what exactly students should be able to do. By creating a list of specific skills, teachers can not only gather data at the individual level but also look across these checklists to identify groups of students who need further instruction. This may include building background knowledge, or simply reteaching. In addition, these teacher-directed small-group arrangements provide the added benefit of having students apply their speaking, listening, and language skills in the service of content.

Formative and Summative Assessments

The usefulness of every assessment is dependent on a proper fit between purpose and type of assessment used. It is important to remember that every assessment is useful and not useful *at the same time*. Any given assessment is useful in the hands of a conscientious educator who understands the limitations of the tool being used. Any given assessment is useless if it is interpreted to show something it was not intended to show. You would be very suspicious of a doctor who ordered a chest x-ray when you were seeking help for a sprained ankle. There is nothing inherently wrong with a chest x-ray, but it is simply the wrong test for the task. In the same regard, the type of reading or writing assessment selected must match its intended use. Andrea Guillaume (2004) offers these considerations for selecting an assessment. Each assessment needs to be:

- Tied to your stance on learning

- Driven by learning goals

- Systematic

- Tied to instruction

- Connected to the learner

- Integrated into a manageable system

Tied to Your Stance on Learning

Every teacher brings a philosophy of education and a view of literacy to his or her practice. It is important to recognize how assessment choices fit into that perspective. For example, an educator who possesses a viewpoint of learning as a developmental phenomenon will be interested in assessment instruments that reflect benchmarks of developmental phases of learning. Teachers with a skills-based orientation will find skills measures to be useful.

Driven by Learning Goals

Classroom assessments should be consistent with the expectations of the grade-level Common Core State Standards. These standards are outcome-based and articulate the *what* of learning. As educators, we must make the decisions about *how* we get there.

Systematic

Teachers select assessments that can be administered and analyzed in a systematic way at both the individual and class levels. Good assessments should possess data recording and analysis protocols that make it easy for the teacher to interpret the information at a later date. In addition, the teacher must determine how often they will be administered. Finally, each assessment should measure what it purports to measure (valid) and yield results that are consistent across administrations and assessors (reliable).

Tied to Instruction

Although this seems apparent, it is worth stating again. Assessment should be linked directly to instruction, either to determine what should be taught next (pretesting) or to check for understanding of skills or strategies that have just been taught (post-testing). Assessments that are not connected to instruction are likely to be frustrating for students because they appear purposeless and inadequate for teachers because they do not provide relevant information.

Connected to the Learner

Assessments are intended to be completed in conjunction with the learners' needs. They should be designed to capture the work of children in the act of learning. Whether through listening to a student reading text (as is the case with running records and informal reading inventories) or using a rubric to discuss a student's writing (analytic writing assessment), these tools are intended to involve the learner in his or her own measures of progress.

Integrated Into a Manageable System

No teacher can devote all his or her time to collecting and analyzing assessment data. The demands of assessment on the time available can become overwhelming and even crowd out equally valuable instructional time. Therefore, it is in the teacher's interest to understand what each assessment does, then select the one that best fits the needs of the students, teacher, and curriculum. The collaborative planning team is the ideal forum for selecting and designing formative assessments that inform instruction.

One of the challenges teachers and teams often encounter with feed-forward systems is creating a manageable system. When teachers evaluate students' work, they often provide individual students with feedback. As we have discussed, this is helpful for the student, and perhaps his or her parents, in understanding areas of strength and need. But it is less helpful for teachers in terms of determining what to teach next. Frankly, it's hard for any of us to remember the range of errors and misconceptions that students have and then to organize instruction around those instructional needs. To effectively implement a formative assessment system, teachers and their collaborative planning teams need to regularly examine student work and identify patterns in the strengths and needs identified in the data.

For example, first-grade teacher Sandy Smalls and her team developed an error-analysis tool with common errors that beginning writers make. They developed this tool so that they could use it in the beginning of the year to determine students' skills and needs (see figure 5.2). They use this tool to analyze students' writing to determine areas of strength and need. The challenge is to figure out what to do with the information once it has been collected. Without some analysis of the patterns that emerge in each classroom, teachers will have a hard time teaching students based on need and are at risk of teaching the whole-class content that some students have already mastered.

Common Errors	Week One	Week Two	Week Three	Week Four	Week Five	Week Six
Letter reversals						
Capital letters in the middle of a word						
Misspellings of grade-level high-frequency words						
Misspellings of grade-level spelling patterns (like *cvc*, *cvc* silent *e*, digraphs *ch*, *th*, *sh*, and *wh*)						
Lowercase letters in the beginning of sentence						
Incorrect ending punctuation						
Improper use of pronouns						
Beginning a sentence with *And*						
Lack of variety at the beginning of sentence						
Lack of clarity in sentence						

Source: Adapted from W. Wells, personal communication, 2012. Used with permission.

Figure 5.2: Sample error analysis for a first-grade writing piece.

Visit **go.solution-tree.com/commoncore** for a reproducible version of this figure.

We recommend that teams develop an error-analysis system that includes all student information on a single sheet of paper. In this case, rather than have the columns for total attempts, correct usage, errors, and percentage of errors, teachers list student initials for those students who have not yet met the standard on any indicator (see figure 5.3).

Common Errors	Students With No Errors	Students With One to Three Errors	Students With Four or More Errors
Letter reversals			
Capital letters in the middle of a word			
Misspellings of grade-level high-frequency words			
Misspellings of grade-level spelling patterns (like *cvc*, *cvc* silent *e*, digraphs *ch*, *th*, *sh*, and *wh*)			
Lowercase letters in the beginning of sentence			
Incorrect ending punctuation			
Improper use of pronouns			
Beginning a sentence with *And*			
Lack of variety at the beginning of sentence			
Lack of clarity in sentence			

Figure 5.3: Revised error analysis for a first-grade writing piece.

Visit **go.solution-tree.com/commoncore** for a reproducible version of this figure.

In one first-grade classroom, three students made excessive errors in misspelling grade-level high-frequency words, a Common Core State Standard that is monitored throughout elementary school. These students need additional instruction, probably small-group instruction, to meet this standard, but the rest of the class does not. The majority of the students in this class made mistakes with grade-level spelling patterns, likely a result of their stage of English language development. As such, the whole class could benefit from instruction in standard English, while also ensuring that they understand that their use of the language is not wrong but rather that there are situations that dictate specific registers and forms of language (Wheeler & Swords, 2006).

If there are specific students who fail to respond to quality core instruction, including the reteaching that comes from careful analysis of student work, the teacher should present this situation and the data that have been collected to the collaborative team for consideration. The team may recommend that an RTI committee evaluate each student, as will be discussed in the next section. Or the team may decide that the student needs to receive some additional instruction from the classroom teacher or from another team member. The key here is to realize that no teacher is alone in this process. Students fail to respond to quality instruction for a whole host of reasons and when groups of teachers get together to problem solve these situations, students benefit. Unfortunately, in some schools, asking other teachers for assistance or advice is seen as a weakness. If we are to implement the Common Core State Standards well, we are going to have to talk and collaborate with our colleagues much more often. Furthermore, we are going to have to talk with them about students who struggle, despite our best efforts to ensure their success.

What to Do When Students Struggle

Sometimes the assessment information that is collected will indicate that a student, or group of students, has failed to make progress. Sometimes this happens because the student did not receive adequate quality core instruction, perhaps due to absences or a specific teaching situation. In that case, the student needs to be retaught the content using evidence-based practices that ensure success. Sometimes students fail to make progress despite solid core instruction. In this case, the student likely needs additional supplemental or intensive intervention. RTI is a system to respond when students fail to progress. As with other efforts to implement the Common Core State Standards, RTI requires the mobilization of collaborative teams and entire school systems (Buffum et al., 2009).

Although RTI has become more broadly known through its inclusion in the Individuals With Disabilities Education Improvement Act of 2004, RTI has existed as a theory and practice for decades. As described in federal legislation, the intent is twofold: (1) to provide early intervention for students who are struggling and (2) to allow for an alternate means of identifying the presence of a learning disability. Unfortunately, in some schools, the latter purpose has overshadowed the former. In an effort to establish a balance between the two, a growing number of states are investing in a response to instruction and intervention (RTI²) model. Before focusing on the major components of an RTI model, we will explore five mistakes that are commonly made when school systems attempt to establish and implement an RTI² program.

Mistake One: Thinking Intervention, Not Instruction

An effective RTI effort begins with a quality core program—this is the first tier of the widely known three-tier model of RTI (for more information, visit the RTI Action Network at www.rtinetwork.org). A quality core program includes the kind of scaffolded learning experiences expressed through a gradual release of responsibility instructional framework (Frey & Fisher, 2010b). This framework includes establishing the purpose of the lesson for students, modeling one's cognitive processes by thinking aloud, and providing guided instruction through the use of questions, prompts, and cues. In addition, students spend much of their time learning collaboratively with their peers in productive group work, before attempting independent learning. Without these practices firmly in place in all classrooms, the supplemental and intensive intervention efforts of any school will be quickly overwhelmed by students who are failing simply because of not receiving quality core instruction.

Consider the practices of first-grade teacher Marci Rivers who skillfully weaves these instructional practices throughout a lesson on the relationship between teeth and diet. She starts with a clear purpose, namely that students will infer an animal's diet based on the shape of its teeth. As part of the lesson, she models her thinking about different types of teeth and what they might be good for, using a document camera to project some sample text. She tells students, "I see some sharp teeth in this illustration. I think that sharp teeth could be useful in eating meat because meat is harder to separate. This one is flatter, so I'm thinking it would be good to grind away at plants." She continues, talking about physical characteristics that help her students understand the animal's diet.

She then invites students to classify different teeth into two categories: (1) plant eaters and (2) meat eaters. She reminds them to discuss their ideas with each other and to use their argumentation skills. She points to a large piece of poster paper that has a number of sentence frames for argumentation, such as the following.

- "I think _____ because _____."
- "I agree with you because _____."
- "I disagree with you because _____."

As groups of students get to work, Ms. Rivers meets with students who have experienced difficulty, as shown in the error-analysis data, this far in the unit for additional guided instruction. They leave their group when she calls them to have a discussion with her. At one point, she meets with three students who have difficulty.

Ms. Rivers says, "Let's take another look at these teeth. Which ones would you say are sharp? Let's start there." Brandon points to the teeth and says, "These three." Christi adds, "Yeah, and this one too." Ms. Rivers agrees and asks, "Yes, these are sharp. What might they be good for in terms of eating?" Randy replies, "I think that they could cut through something, like a knife." Brandon chimes in, "Yeah, like meat, when you cut it." Ms. Rivers comments, "You're right. These are sharp so they are probably useful for animals that eat meat." Christi asks, "But could they work for plants too?" Ms. Rivers responds, "Yes, and we're going to talk about animals that eat both meat and plants."

As they work with their teacher, these three students are developing an increased understanding of the content such that they have sufficient background knowledge to read the textbook. In the meantime, the other students in the classroom are sorting information and applying new vocabulary words—*carnivore* and *herbivore*—to their charts. If these three students do not make progress, their teacher will discuss their needs with her collaborative planning team, and the team may recommend that they receive Tier 2 or Tier 3 interventions. At this point, however, their learning needs are being exposed through formative assessments that provide Ms. Rivers with information about their learning needs.

Mistake Two: Relying on Prepackaged Curricula

While commercial programs labeled as being intervention friendly can provide some needed practice materials, they cannot replace well-designed and individualized lessons targeting the specific needs of students who require intervention. Second-grade teacher James Perry accesses the resources of Margaret Ingraham, a reading specialist who provides supplemental and intensive interventions.

As Mr. Perry notes, "I know that my students receive support that they need to learn the content of second grade. This includes some basic skills, but also the content that our class is studying. If we just bought a program, it would probably not help with all of the specific informational texts that I use in the class for science and social studies." Rebecca, a student in Mr. Perry's classroom, is fortunate to attend a school that has avoided the error of relying exclusively on commercial programs for intervention.

"We used to drag all the Tier 2 students through the same reading program, regardless of their needs," says reading specialist Ms. Ingraham. "Now I align my materials with what students are using in their classrooms." Rebecca, who struggles with reading comprehension, reads passages from her textbooks and other related texts.

"I know from talking with Mr. Perry that Rebecca's class is studying life cycles right now, so the vocabulary and reading work that we're doing together right now is about that," says Ms. Ingraham. She counts on regular communication with the other teachers to design lessons that are meaningful.

Mistake Three: Isolating Teachers and Interventionists

Coordinating learning across the school day is challenging under the best of circumstances, and adding intervention efforts to the mix can be difficult. It can be tempting to simply put one teacher in charge of an RTI program, give him or her a classroom, and turn attention to other matters. But isolating interventionists from classroom teachers severely limits the kind of collaboration Ms. Ingraham and Mr. Perry are able to accomplish for Rebecca's benefit. Instead, consider the team effort each student in an RTI[2] program will need to be successful. It is important to make sure that every student receiving supplemental or intensive interventions has an identified person coordinating instruction and another coordinating intervention. Communication between these two educators can bridge the divide that can otherwise occur when interventions are disconnected from the core curriculum.

Mistake Four: Making Data Decisions Alone

Ms. Ingraham, Rebecca's intervention teacher, collects data each time she meets with the student so that she can track progress and determine what is working. Importantly, data collection and analysis also reveal when something is not working. "I initially started out with using timed writing with Rebecca, but I quickly discovered that wasn't the best approach. I found that when I gave her a chance to discuss the reading with me for a few minutes first, her writing improved in length and content," says Ms. Ingraham.

Both Mr. Perry and Ms. Ingraham serve on the school's RTI^2 subcommittee, an outgrowth of the Student Study Team formed to closely examine the circumstances surrounding specific students' behavioral or academic difficulties. The subcommittee meets regularly to discuss the progress of students receiving intervention supports. Ms. Ingraham brings her data to the group for discussion and finds that others can sometimes spot a trend she had overlooked. In addition, she can share her insights about what she has found effective. For instance, she recommends that Mr. Perry encourage Shannon to plan her writing orally in advance of extended writing assignments. "I've been more conscious of doing this for the last few weeks," Ms. Ingraham observes, "and I'm seeing that it's giving her a chance to organize her thoughts better. Her writing is beginning to improve."

Mistake Five: Leaving the Family Out of the Planning

Family involvement is key when students who struggle are participating in RTI^2 efforts. In fact, the family may possess quite a bit of information that can be helpful in determining ways to accelerate student learning. As keepers of their child's history, family members have firsthand knowledge about what has worked in the past. However, this information can come too late in the process when families are contacted only after a student's lack of RTI warrants a referral for special education testing. It is understandable that families can become justifiably frustrated when they learn that their child has been involved in an intervention for months without their knowledge.

At Rebecca's school, her mother and grandmother meet with the administrator who oversees the RTI^2 program. Ms. Ingraham explains why Rebecca is being recommended for supplemental intervention and gathers information from them about past efforts. Ms. Ingraham speaks with them on the phone each month to share Rebecca's progress and asks them about their observations. Rebecca's eventual progress means that she doesn't require a referral for special education testing; the school gains two important allies. "I was caught a little off guard when the school called me," Rebecca's grandmother says. "After all, she'd only been there for a few weeks." The girl's mother continues. "But we really got to see how much the school cares about Rebecca's progress. It's good to know she's noticed, even at a busy school."

Assessment, Intervention, and Instruction

Second-grade teacher Amanda Thibodeau regularly collects formative assessment information for all of her students in order to ensure they are receiving appropriate instruction. She tracks her observations and keeps a record of formal assessment results. She often uses her conferring time during independent activities as a time to collect and record further individual assessment information. One student has been worrying her. Ahmed is an English learner, who has various needs in speaking, reading, and writing as he continues to learn the English language. She further describes Ahmed as extremely shy. "I need to help him open up, make friends, and feel more comfortable taking risks." Some of this is due to his status as an English learner. He is at the intermediate stage of language development. "I always need to keep in mind that I have to compare English learners to true peers, and not let his chronological age alone be the only metric I use," she says.

Ahmed knows how to use his resources when he is stuck, which is a major strength as students move into third grade and beyond. He uses the teacher's assistance as his last resort to finding an answer to a question, and he is highly motivated and maintains a positive attitude in the classroom. His peers respect him and welcome him into social groups in the classroom. Although he has many strengths and positive aspects, Ahmed has needs related to his language development and vocabulary. Because his English proficiency is at the intermediate stage, Ahmed needs specific help in order to improve his language development. Ahmed also needs help in reading and writing. He uses the resources Ms. Thibodeau has created with him such as personal dictionaries, the word wall, and other resources based on a particular lesson or unit of study. But despite a good attitude and some additional supports as a language learner, his progress has stalled. Ms. Thibodeau decides that the first place to begin is with some individual assessments.

Assessment

Ms. Thibodeau begins by revisiting the assessments she already had done with Ahmed. For example, she administered an informal reading inventory at the beginning of the school year. In addition, she had the state language assessment for English learners. The results suggested that Ahmed needs to focus on vocabulary and writing.

Ms. Thibodeau continues by collecting a timed writing sample and uses both a holistic rubric and an analytic writing tool to gain a more detailed view of his on-demand writing. From her analysis of this data, she also notes that Ahmed still needs help with spelling, paragraph development, and vocabulary enhancement. It is also clear that Ahmed has complex thoughts, but has difficulty communicating exactly what he wants to say.

She also data collected informally during whole-class lessons and small-group sessions using an error-analysis protocol her team had developed for small-group discussions. For example, Ms. Thibodeau notes that during guided reading, Ahmed reads quietly and is somewhat reserved. He chooses to participate, but rarely contributes to the discussion. When Ms. Thibodeau uses a retelling inventory, she writes that Ahmed can identify some of the main ideas, but cannot provide many story details. He is also unable to use evidence from the text, even when prompted.

Ms. Thibodeau also remarks that examining a student's homework or independent practice component of a lesson is a great way to see if a student is understanding the material. As she says, "Homework is a wonderful assessment tool because the students are required to apply previously taught information. It's not the stuff they are currently learning. But it's content they learned earlier this school year; even last year. If students can apply learned concepts to an independent homework assignment in a different environment in which they learned it, they have mastered the concepts." When she reviews Ahmed's homework, she finds that while he tries to complete most of these assignments, few of them are done accurately.

Intervention

Based on her findings, she takes the data she analyzes to her next collaborative planning team meeting. She describes Ahmed's lack of progress in some areas and offers evidence of his strengths as well. The team provides reflective feedback and invites her to speculate about possible solutions. The discussion proves to be a moment of clarity for her. "He's an English learner, and some of his difficulties might be explained by that. But it's his lack of progress since the beginning of this year that's so troublesome. It's time to move into some Tier 2 supplemental instruction."

Ms. Thibodeau consults with the school's English learner specialist, Janet Hall, to design supplemental instruction for Ahmed. Together they make a plan for daily additional small-group instruction with two other students. "I wanted to make sure there were other people he had to talk to," Ms. Thibodeau says. The daily lesson format began with a making words activity. Based on her assessment information, Ms. Thibodeau knows that Ahmed sometimes has trouble with correctly identifying letter domains, which greatly impacts his spelling. Her anecdotal notes indicate that Ahmed was pretty successful at this activity because he found the pattern in the word families. Ahmed found the letter-sound patterns almost immediately while some students struggled making the words correctly.

Instruction

She monitors his progress by using a developmental spelling inventory. Because Ahmed catches on rapidly, Ms. Thibodeau alters her objectives for this supplemental intervention after several weeks and focuses on transferring his learning to writing in content areas. "I didn't stop with having him make words and sort them," she explains. "But I found what worked, and I shifted those activities to his Tier 1 guided instruction." Ms. Hall looks at the results of the teacher's progress-monitoring data and agrees.

Because Ahmed also needs writing instruction, Ms. Thibodeau decides to make this the focus of her conferring time. She creates a lesson using a children's thesaurus to increase Ahmed's vocabulary to *superstar* words rather than just *regular* words. For example, Ms. Thibodeau helps Ahmed look up the word *happy* and select a superstar word. In this case, he selects *joyful*.

The use of the thesaurus is helpful for Ahmed when the students write opinion pieces about a new piece of playground equipment. Her analysis of his writing reveals that rather than using simple words like he did in his opinion piece from earlier in the year, Ahmed is now using more complex vocabulary because he looks up the words he wants to use in a thesaurus to find other words that mean the same thing.

Ahmed receives Tier 2 supplemental intervention for several months. The goal isn't to rapidly eliminate any traces of the learning progression of someone still learning a new language. Rather, Ms. Thibodeau is alarmed that his learning slowed and she needed more time with him to figure out what could work. "He didn't need Tier 2 supplemental intervention because I was worried about him having a disability," she remarks. "I knew he needed more instruction, and I needed to be more effective than I was. Really, it was a win-win situation for both of us."

Conclusion

To fully operationalize the information in this chapter, collaborative teams must develop their assessment literacy (Boudett, City, & Murnane, 2005). In other words, they need to know which assessment tools work for which tasks and in which ways. Furthermore, teams in collaboration with site leadership should develop an assessment calendar so that all members of the school community know which assessments they should give, and when. Once the more formal assessment system has been developed, the team can then turn its attention to monitoring student progress. This occurs on many levels, ranging from the analysis of state assessments to reviews of student work. Regardless of the level, the collaborative team should be on the lookout for students who are not responding to quality core instruction. In these cases, the team needs to discuss ways to ensure that students are supported, including through informal reteaching and formal response to intervention systems. Highly effective collaborative planning teams have data management systems for keeping track of students as they progress through the year and early warning systems that provide alerts when students are not making progress.

This chapter has focused on the many kinds of assessment instruments available to classroom teachers in order to plan instruction, monitor growth, and evaluate learning. However, as we stated previously, no one assessment is ideal for every situation. As the teacher and member of a collaborative planning team, you will need to determine what kinds of information you need about your students, which instruments can give you the information you are seeking, and how much time you have available to administer and analyze. Therefore, we believe that the assessments themselves need to be analyzed to see which best fit your purposes. Every time you consider a new assessment, we encourage you to ask yourself the following questions.

- **"What does this assessment really measure?"** Don't let the title of the assessment fool you. Look closely at the task demands to make sure that other skills like reading, writing, or using language don't confound results.

- **"What will the results tell me? What will the results *not* tell me?"** Make sure that the information an assessment yields is necessary and is not duplicated by another assessment. Also, be clear about what other assessments you might need to administer in order to give a more complete picture of a learner.

- **"What expenditure of my time and effort will be required to administer and analyze the assessment?"** The time you have available is finite. Some assessments are time consuming to administer but yield rich results that make them worthwhile. Others are quick but may deliver little in the way of useable information. Plan your assessment calendar like you do your curricular one to ensure you are using your time (and your students') wisely.

- **"How will this assessment help my instruction?"** A New Zealand proverb says, "You don't fatten sheep by weighing them." We are concerned about the increase in the amount of testing that is occurring in schools in the name of accountability. Instructional time is increasingly being whittled away in order to do more testing. This chapter has focused on classroom assessments that translate to instructional decisions. When chosen wisely and analyzed with care, these assessments ultimately save instructional time by allowing the teacher to be more precise in choosing what to teach, what to reteach, and when the student can move on to new content.

- **"How can this assessment figure into my intervention efforts and reporting requirements?"** Not every assessment is suitable for such determinations, as some are diagnostic and others are used for accountability. However, the majority of assessments should provide information about next steps for instruction and the possible need for intervention. In addition, these assessments should help inform the team about the effectiveness of the intervention efforts, known as *progress monitoring,* and can also be helpful in parent and student conferences as well as reporting successes and needs on report cards.

The Common Core State Standards for English language arts present an opportunity for teachers and their teams to collaborate in ways that result in improved student achievement. These standards represent a shift as well as an increase in expectations, and our students deserve nothing less than our very best effort to ensure that they meet these standards so they are prepared for the next stage in their life, middle school, high school, and beyond.

REFERENCES AND RESOURCES

Abbott, R. D., Berninger, V. M., & Fayol, M. (2010). Longitudinal relationships of levels of language in writing and between writing and reading in grades 1 and 7. *Journal of Educational Psychology, 102*(2), 281–298.

Adler, M. J., & Van Doren, C. (1972). *How to read a book*. New York: Touchstone.

Aliki. (1988). *Digging up dinosaurs* (Rev. ed.). New York: Cromwell.

Aliki. (1989). *My five senses*. New York: HarperCollins.

Aliki. (1990). *Fossils tell of long ago* (Rev. ed.). New York: Cromwell.

Allington, R. L. (2002). You can't learn much from books you can't read. *Educational Leadership, 60*(3), 16–19.

American Library Association. (2012). *Terms and criteria: Randolph Caldecott medal*. Accessed at www.ala.org/alsc/awardsgrants/bookmedia/caldecottmedal /caldecottterms/caldecottterms on May 23, 2012.

American Speech-Language-Hearing Association. (2012). *What is language? What is speech?* Accessed at www.asha.org/public/speech/development/language _speech.htm on May 23, 2012.

Arnold, T. (2005). *Hi! Fly guy*. New York: Scholastic.

Aronsky, J. (2008). *Wild tracks! A guide to nature's footprints*. New York: Sterling.

Ashton-Warner, S. (1965). *Teacher*. New York: Simon & Schuster.

Baumann, J. (2009). Vocabulary and reading comprehension. In S. E. Israel & G. G. Duffy (Eds.), *Handbook of research on reading comprehension* (pp. 323–346). New York: Routledge.

Baumann, J. F., Font, G., Edwards, E. C., & Boland, E. (2005). Strategies for teaching middle-grade students to use word-part and context clues to expand reading vocabulary. In E. H. Hiebert & M. L. Kamil (Eds.), *Teaching and learning vocabulary: Bringing research to practice* (pp. 179–205). Mahwah, NJ: Erlbaum.

Bayliss, V. A. (1994). Fluency in children's writing. *Reading Horizons, 34*(3), 247–256.

Bayliss, V. A., & Walker, N. L. (1988). *Bayliss/Walker scales: Holistic writing evaluation, grades 1–6.* Springfield: Southwest Missouri State University.

Bear, D. R., Invernizzi, M. R., Templeton, S., & Johnston, F. R. (2012). *Words their way: Word study for phonics, vocabulary, and spelling instruction* (5th ed.). Boston: Allyn & Bacon.

Beck, I. L., McKeown, M. G., & Kucan, L. (2002). *Bringing words to life: Robust vocabulary instruction.* New York: Guilford Press.

Beck, I. L., McKeown, M. G., & Kucan, L. (2008). *Creating robust vocabulary: Frequently asked questions and extended examples.* New York: Guilford Press.

Beers, S. F., & Nagy, W. E. (2011). Writing development in four genres from grades three to seven: Syntactic complexity and genre differentiation. *Reading & Writing Quarterly, 24,* 183–202.

Berninger, V. M., & Abbott, R. D. (2010). Listening comprehension, oral expression, reading comprehension, and written expression: Related yet unique language systems in grades 1, 3, 5, and 7. *Journal of Educational Psychology, 102*(3), 635–651.

Biemiller, A. (2005). Size and sequence in vocabulary development: Implications for choosing words for primary grade vocabulary instruction. In E. H. Hiebert & M. L. Kamil (Eds.), *Teaching and learning vocabulary: Bringing research to practice* (pp. 223–242). Mahwah, NJ: Erlbaum.

Birenbaum, M., Kimron, H., & Shilton, H. (2011). Nested contexts that shape assessment for learning: School-based professional learning community and classroom culture. *Studies in Educational Evaluation, 37*(1), 35–48.

Blachowicz, C., & Fisher, P. (2002). *Teaching vocabulary in all classrooms* (2nd ed.). Upper Saddle River, NJ: Merrill/Prentice Hall.

Bossert, T. S., & Schwantes, F. M. (1995). Children's comprehension monitoring: Training children to use rereading to aid comprehension. *Reading Research and Instruction, 35*(2), 109–121.

Boudett, K. P., City, E. A., & Murnane, R. J. (Eds.). (2005). *Data wise: A step-by-step guide to using assessment results to improve teaching and learning.* Cambridge, MA: Harvard Education Press.

Bransford, J. D., Brown, A. L., & Cocking, R. R. (Eds). (2000). *How people learn: Brain, mind, experience, and school.* Washington, DC: National Academy Press.

Britton, J. (1983). Writing and the story of the world. In B. M. Kroll & G. Wells (Eds.), *Explorations in the development of writing: Theory, research, and practice* (pp. 3–30). New York: Wiley.

Buffum, A., Mattos, M., & Weber, C. (2009). *Pyramid response to intervention: RTI, professional learning communities, and how to respond when kids don't learn.* Bloomington, IN: Solution Tree Press.

Bullough, R. V., Jr., & Baugh, S. C. (2008). Building professional learning communities within a university–public school partnership. *Theory Into Practice, 47*(4), 286–293.

Bunting, E. (1994). *Smoky night.* San Diego, CA: Harcourt.

Cahill, M., & Gregory, A. E. (2011). Putting the fun back into fluency instruction. *The Reading Teacher, 65*(2), 127–131.

Callison, D., & Preddy, L. (2006). *The blue book on Information Age inquiry, instruction, and literacy.* Santa Barbara, CA: Libraries Unlimited.

Carle, E. (1969). *The very hungry caterpillar.* New York: Philomel Books.

Carlson, C. (2000). Scientific literacy for all. *Science Teacher, 67*(3), 48–52.

Cazden, C. B. (2001). *Classroom discourse: The language of teaching and learning* (2nd ed.). Portsmouth, NH: Heinemann.

Chall, J. S., Conard, S., & Harris, S. H. (1977). *An analysis of textbooks in relation to declining SAT scores: Prepared for the advisory panel on the Scholastic Aptitude Test score decline.* Princeton, NJ: College Board Publication Orders.

Chall, J. S., & Jacobs, V. A. (2003). Poor children's fourth-grade slump. *American Educator, 27*(1), 14–15, 44.

Christelow, E. (1989). *Five little monkeys jumping on the bed.* New York: Clarion Books.

Clay, M. M. (2000). *Concepts about print: What have children learned about the way we print language?* Portsmouth, NH: Heinemann.

Clay, M. M. (2002). *An observation survey of early literacy achievement* (2nd ed.). Portsmouth, NH: Heinemann.

Coker, D. (2007). Writing instruction for young children. In S. Graham, C. A. MacArthur, & J. Fitzgerald (Eds.), *Best practices in writing instruction* (pp. 101–118). New York: Guilford Press.

Consortium on Reading Excellence. (1999). *Assessing reading: Multiple measures for kindergarten through eighth grade.* Novato, CA: Arena Press.

Council of Chief State School Officers. (2012, January 26). *The Common Core State Standards: Supporting districts and teachers with text complexity* [Video webcast]. Accessed at https://ccsso.webex.com/mw0306ld/mywebex/default .do;jsessionid=KGRNPd6hnnshndyz9QLk5qthTtFvV6yPkQTTPg2XGvZ48 9Lm2pTQ!1006560109?nomenu=true&siteurl=ccsso&service=6&rnd=0.8424 170944354614&main_url=https%3A%2F%2Fccsso.webex.com%2Fec0605ld %2Feventcenter%2Fprogram%2FprogramDetail.do%3FtheAction%3Ddetail %26siteurl%3Dccsso%26cProgViewID%3D22 on May 24, 2012.

Cowley, J. (1989). *Baby gets dressed.* New York: Wright Group/McGraw-Hill.

Cowley, J. (1998). *Meanies.* New York: Wright Group/McGraw-Hill.

Crain, W. C. (2000). *Theories of development: Concepts and applications* (4th ed.). Upper Saddle River, NJ: Prentice Hall.

Crews, D. (1980). *Truck.* New York: Greenwillow Books.

Csikszentmihalyi, M. (1997). *Finding flow: The psychology of engagement with everyday life.* New York: Basic Books.

Csikszentmihalyi, M. (2000). *Beyond boredom and anxiety: Experiencing flow in work and play.* San Francisco: Jossey-Bass.

Cutler, L., & Graham, S. (2008). Primary grade writing instruction: A national survey. *Journal of Educational Psychology, 100*(4), 909–919.

Daniels, P. (1999). *Oceans.* Washington, DC: National Geographic Society.

Darling-Hammond, L. (2010). *The flat world and education: How America's commitment to equity will determine our future.* New York: Teachers College Press.

Dorn, L. J., & Soffos, C. (2001). *Scaffolding young writers: A writers' workshop approach.* Portland, ME: Stenhouse.

DuFour, R., DuFour, R., & Eaker, R. (2008). *Revisiting professional learning communities at work: New insights for improving schools.* Bloomington, IN: Solution Tree Press.

DuFour, R., DuFour, R., Eaker, R., & Many, T. (2010). *Learning by doing: A handbook for professional learning communities at work™* (2nd ed.). Bloomington, IN: Solution Tree Press.

DuFour, R., & Marzano, R. J. (2011). *Leaders of learning: How district, school, and classroom leaders improve student achievement.* Bloomington, IN: Solution Tree Press.

Duke, N. K. (2000). 3.6 minutes per day: The scarcity of informational texts in first grade. *Reading Research Quarterly, 35*(2), 202–224.

Duke, N. K., & Roberts, K. M. (2010). The genre-specific nature of reading comprehension. In D. Wyse, R. Andrews, & J. Hoffman (Eds.). *The Routledge International Handbook of English Language and Literacy Teaching* (pp. 74–86). London: Routledge.

Eaker, R., DuFour, R., & DuFour, R. (2002). *Getting started: Reculturing schools to become professional learning communities.* Bloomington, IN: Solution Tree Press.

Elbow, P. (1981). *Writing with power: Techniques for mastering the writing process.* New York: Oxford University Press.

Fearn, L., & Farnan, N. (2001). *Interactions: Teaching writing and the language arts.* Boston: Houghton Mifflin.

Fisher, D., & Frey, N. (2007a). *Scaffolding writing instruction: A gradual-release framework.* New York: Scholastic Teaching Resources.

Fisher, D., & Frey, N. (2007b). *Checking for understanding: Formative assessment techniques for your classroom.* Alexandria, VA: Association for Supervision and Curriculum Development.

Fisher, D., & Frey, N. (2010). *Enhancing RTI: How to ensure success with effective classroom instruction and intervention.* Alexandria, VA: Association for Supervision and Curriculum Development.

Fisher, D., Frey, N., & Lapp, D. (2012). *Text complexity: Raising rigor in reading.* Newark, DE: International Reading Association.

Fleischman, P. (1988). Fireflies. In *Joyful noise: Poems for two voices* (pp. 11–14). New York: HarperCollins.

Flood, J., Lapp, D., & Fisher, D. (2005). Neurological impress method plus. *Reading Psychology, 26,* 147–160.

Freeman, D. (2002). *Gregory's shadow.* New York: Puffin.

Frey, N., & Fisher, D. (2007). *Reading for information in elementary school: Content literacy strategies to build comprehension.* Upper Saddle River, NJ: Merrill Prentice Hall.

Frey, N., & Fisher, D. (2009). *Learning words inside and out: Vocabulary instruction that boosts achievement in all subject areas.* Portsmouth, NH: Heinemann.

Frey, N., & Fisher, D. (2010a). Reading and the brain: What early childhood educators need to know. *Early Childhood Education Journal, 38*(2), 103–110.

Frey, N., & Fisher, D. (2010b). Getting to quality: A meeting of the minds. *Principal Leadership, 11*(1), 68–70.

Frey, N., & Fisher, D. (2011). *The formative assessment action plan: Practical steps to more successful teaching and learning.* Alexandria, VA: Association for Supervision and Curriculum Development.

Frey, N., Fisher, D., & Berkin, A. (2008). *Good habits, great readers: Building the literacy community.* Upper Saddle River, NJ: Allyn & Bacon.

Frey, N., Fisher, D., & Everlove, S. (2009). *Productive group work: How to engage students, build teamwork, and promote understanding.* Alexandria, VA: Association for Supervision and Curriculum Development.

Frey, N., Fisher, D., & Gonzalez, A. (2010). *Literacy 2.0: Reading and writing in 21st century classrooms.* Bloomington, IN: Solution Tree Press.

Frey, N., Fisher, D., & Nelson, J. (2010). Lessons scooped from the melting pot: California district increases achievement through English language development. *Journal of Staff Development, 31*(5), 24–28.

Gamoran, A. (2007). *Standards-based reform and the poverty gap: Lessons from No Child Left Behind.* Washington, DC: Brookings Institution.

Ganske, K. (2000). *Word journeys: Assessment-guided phonics, spelling, and vocabulary instruction*. New York: Guilford Press.

Ganske, L. (1981). Note-taking: A significant and integral part of learning environments. *Educational Communication and Technology: A Journal of Theory, Research, and Development, 29*, 155–175.

Garza, C. L. (2005). *Family pictures/Cuadros de familia*. San Francisco: Children's Book Press.

Gee, J. P. (1996). *Social linguistics and literacies: Ideology in discourses* (2nd ed.). London: Taylor & Francis.

Gentry, J. R. (2006). *Breaking the code: The new science of beginning reading and writing*. Portsmouth, NH: Heinemann.

Ghiso, M. (2011). "Writing that matters": Collaborative inquiry and authoring practices in a first-grade class. *Language Arts, 88*(5), 346–355.

Gibbons, G. (1991a). *From seed to plant*. New York: Holiday House.

Gibbons, G. (1991b). *Monarch butterfly*. New York: Holiday House.

Giovanni, N. (1990). Covers. In J. Prelutsky (Ed.), *The 20th century children's poetry treasury* (p. 85). New York: Knopf. (Original work published 1980)

Graves, M. F., & Watts-Taffe, S. M. (2002). The place of word consciousness in a research-based vocabulary program. In A. E. Farstrup & S. J. Samuels (Eds.), *What research has to say about reading instruction* (3rd ed.; pp. 140–165). Newark, DE: International Reading Association.

Guillaume, A. M. (2004). *K–12 classroom teaching: A primer for new professionals* (2nd ed.). Upper Saddle River, NJ: Pearson/Merrill/Prentice Hall.

Harste, J. C., Woodward, V. A., & Burke, C. L. (1984). *Language stories and literacy lessons*. Portsmouth, NH: Heinemann Educational.

Hattie, J., & Timperley, H. (2007). The power of feedback. *Review of Educational Research, 77*(1), 81–112.

Hayes, A. (1995). *Meet the orchestra*. New York: Sandpiper.

Hayes, D. P., Wolfer, L. T., & Wolfe, M. (1996). Sourcebook simplification and its relation to the decline in SAT-Verbal scores. *American Educational Research Journal, 33*(2), 489–508.

Henderson, E. (1985). *Teaching spelling*. Boston: Houghton Mifflin.

Henkes, K. (2004). *Kitten's first full moon*. New York: Greenwillow Books.

Hoban, T. (1987). *I read signs*. New York: HarperCollins.

Hodgkins, F., & Kelley, T. (2007). *How people learned to fly*. New York: HarperCollins.

Howell, W. C. (2002). *Zoo flakes ABC*. New York: Walker.

Hurd, E. T. (1962). *Starfish*. New York: HarperCollins.

Individuals With Disabilities Education Act, 20 U.S.C. § 1400 (2004).

Individuals With Disabilities Education Improvement Act of 2004, Pub. L. No. 108-446, 118 Stat. 2647.

Jalongo, M. R., & Sobolak, M. J. (2011). Supporting young children's vocabulary growth: The challenges, the benefits, and evidence-based strategies. *Early Childhood Education Journal, 38*(6), 421–429.

Jenkins, S., & Page, R. (2003). *What do you do with a tail like this?* Orlando, FL: Houghton Mifflin.

Jeong, J., Gaffney, J. S., & Choi, J. (2010). Availability and use of informational texts in second-, third-, and fourth-grade classrooms. *Research in the Teaching of English, 44*(4), 435–456.

Johnston, F. R., Bear, D. R., Invernizzi, M. R., & Templeton, S. (2009). *Words their way: Word sorts for letter name-alphabetic spellers* (2nd ed.). Upper Saddle River, NJ: Prentice Hall.

Johnston, F. R., Invernizzi, M. R., Bear, D. R., & Templeton, S. (2008). *Words their way sorts for syllable and affix spellers* (2nd ed.). Upper Saddle River, NJ: Prentice Hall.

Johnson, S. T. (1995). *Alphabet city*. New York: Puffin.

Joyce, B., & Showers, B. (1983). *Power in staff development through research on training*. Washington, DC: Association for Supervision and Curriculum Development.

Kanold, T., Briars, D., & Fennell, F. (2012). *What principals need to know about teaching and learning mathematics*. Bloomington, IN: Solution Tree Press.

Kim, Y. S., Otaiba, S. A., Puranik, C., Folsom, J. S., Guerlich, L., & Wagner, R. K. (2011). Componential skills of beginning writing: An exploratory study. *Learning and Individual Differences, 21*(5), 517–525.

Kluth, P., & Kluth, V. (2010). *A is for "all aboard!"* Baltimore: Brookes.

Kress, G. (1999). Genre and the changing contexts for English language arts. *Language Arts, 76*(6), 461–469.

Kroll, S. (1995). *It's groundhog day!* New York: Scholastic.

LaMarche, J. (2000). *The raft*. New York: HarperCollins.

Langer, J. A. (1986). *Children reading and writing: Structures and strategies*. Norwood, NJ: Ablex.

Langstaff, J. (1800/1973). *Over in the meadow*. Orlando: Houghton Mifflin.

Lapp, D., Fisher, D., Flood, J., & Cabello, A. (2001). An integrated approach to the teaching and assessment of language arts. In S. R. Hurley & J. V. Tinajero (Eds.), *Literacy assessment of second language learners* (pp. 1–26). Boston: Allyn & Bacon.

Leithwood, K., McAdie, P., Bascia, N. & Rodrigue, A. (Eds.). (2006). *Teaching for deep understanding: What every educator should know.* Thousand Oaks, CA: Corwin Press.

Lennon, C., & Burdick, H. (2004). *The Lexile Framework as an approach for reading measurement and success: A white paper from the Lexile Framework for Reading.* Accessed at www.lexile.com/m/uploads/whitepapers/Lexile-Reading-Measurement -and-Success-0504_MetaMetricsWhitepaper.pdf on July 23, 2012.

Littleton, E. B. (1998). Emerging cognitive skills for writing: Sensitivity to audience presence in five- through nine-year-olds' speech. *Cognition and Instruction, 16*(4), 399–430.

Lobel, A. (1999). *Frog and toad together.* New York: HarperCollins.

Lyons, C., & Pinnell, G. S. (2001). *Systems for change in literacy education: A guide to professional development.* Portsmouth, NH: Heinemann.

MacGillivray, L., & Hawes, S. (1994). "I don't know what I'm doing, they all start with 'B'": Children negotiating peer reading interactions. *The Reading Teacher, 48*, 210–217.

Manzo, A. (1969). ReQuest: A method for improving reading comprehension through reciprocal questioning. *Journal of Reading, 12*(3), 123–126.

Martinez, M., Roser, N., & Strecker, S. (1999). "I never thought I could be a star": A readers' theater ticket to fluency. *The Reading Teacher, 52*, 326–334.

McCarrier, A., Pinnell, G. S., & Fountas, I. C. (2000). *Interactive writing: How language and literacy come together, K–2.* Portsmouth, NH: Heinemann.

McCutcheon, D., Covill, A., Hoyne, S. H., & Mildes, K. (1994). Individual differences in writing: Implications of translating fluency. *Journal of Educational Psychology, 86*(2), 256–266.

Michaels, S., O'Connor, C., & Resnick, L. B. (2008). Deliberative discourse idealized and realized: Accountable talk in the classroom and in civic life. *Studies in Philosophy and Education, 27*(4), 283–297.

Miller, C. R. (1984). Genre as social action. *Quarterly Journal of Speech, 70*(2), 151–167.

Moore, N., & MacArthur, C. (2012). The effects of being a reader and of observing readers on fifth-grade students' argumentative writing and revising. *Reading & Writing, 25*(6), 1449–1478.

Morris, A. (1995). *Shoes, shoes, shoes.* New York: Mulberry Books.

Moss, B. (2003). *Exploring the literature of fact: Children's nonfiction trade books in the elementary classroom.* New York: Guilford Press.

Moss, B. (2004). Teaching expository text structures through informational trade book retellings. *The Reading Teacher, 57,* 710–179.

Moss, B. (2005). Making a case and a place for effective content area literacy instruction in the elementary grades. *The Reading Teacher, 59,* 46–55.

Moss, L. (2000): *Zin! Zin! Zin! A violin.* New York: Simon & Schuster.

Mueller, A., & Fleming, T. (2001). Cooperative learning: Listening to how children work at school. *Journal of Educational Research, 94,* 259–265.

Nagin, C. (2003). *Because writing matters: Improving student writing in our schools.* San Francisco: Jossey-Bass.

Nagy, W. E., & Scott, J. A. (2000). Vocabulary processes. In M. L. Kamil, P. B. Mosenthal, P. D. Pearson, & R. Barr (Eds.), *Handbook of reading research* (Vol. 3; pp. 269–284). Mahwah, NJ: Erlbaum.

National Educational Goals Panel. (1998). *Ready schools.* Washington, DC: Author.

National Governors Association Center for Best Practices & Council of Chief State School Officers. (2010a). *Common Core State Standards for English language arts & literacy in history/social studies, science, and technical subjects.* Washington, DC: Authors. Accessed at www.corestandards.org/assets/CCSSI _ELA%20Standards.pdf on February 10, 2012.

National Governors Association Center for Best Practices & Council of Chief State School Officers. (2010b). *Common Core State Standards for English language arts & literacy in history/social studies, science, and technical subjects: Appendix A—Research supporting key elements of the standards.* Washington, DC: Authors. Accessed at www.corestandards.org/assets/Appendix_A.pdf on February 10, 2012.

National Governors Association Center for Best Practices & Council of Chief State School Officers. (2010c). *Common Core State Standards for English language arts & literacy in history/social studies, science, and technical subjects: Appendix B—Text exemplars and sample performance tasks.* Washington, DC: Authors. Accessed at www.corestandards.org/assets/Appendix_B.pdf on February 10, 2012.

National Governors Association Center for Best Practices & Council of Chief State School Officers. (2010d). *Common Core State Standards for English language arts & literacy in history/social studies, science, and technical subjects: Appendix C—Samples of student writing.* Washington, DC: Authors. Accessed at www .corestandards.org/assets/Appendix_C.pdf on February 10, 2012.

National Governors Association Center for Best Practices & Council of Chief State School Officers. (2010e). *Common Core State Standards for mathematics.* Washington, DC: Authors. Accessed at www.corestandards.org/assets/CCSSI _Math%20Standards.pdf on July 16, 2012.

National Institute of Child Health and Human Development. (2000). *Report of the National Reading Panel: Teaching children to read—An evidence-based assessment of the scientific research literature on reading and its implications for reading instruction* (NIH Publication No. 00–4769). Washington, DC: U.S. Government Printing Office.

National Research Council. (1996). *National Science Education Standards: Observe, interact, change, learn.* Washington, DC: National Academies Press.

National Writing Project, & Nagin, C. (2003). *Because writing matters: Improving student writing in our schools.* San Francisco: Jossey-Bass.

Nelson, R. (2003). *Transportation: Then and now.* Minneapolis, MN: Lerner.

Padak, N., Bromley, K., Rasinski, T., & Newton, E. (2012). Vocabulary: Five common misconceptions. *Educational Leadership Online, 69.* Accessed at www.ascd.org/publications/educational-leadership/jun12/vol69/num09/Vocabulary@-Five-Common-Misconceptions.aspx on July 25, 2012.

Paris, S. G. (2005). Reinterpreting the development of reading skills. *Reading Research Quarterly, 40*(2), 184–202.

Park, B. (1992). *Junie B. Jones and the stupid, smelly bus.* New York: Random House.

Pauk, W. (1974). *How to study in college.* Boston: Houghton Mifflin.

Pearson, P. D., & Gallagher, M. C. (1983). The instruction of reading comprehension. *Contemporary Educational Psychology, 8*(3), 317–344.

Pinczes, E. J. (1993). *One hundred hungry ants.* Boston: Houghton Mifflin.

Popham, W. J. (2008). *Transformative assessment.* Alexandria, VA: Association for Supervision and Curriculum Development.

Porter, A., McMaken, J., Hwang, J., & Yang, R. (2011). Common Core standards: The new U.S. intended curriculum. *Educational Researcher, 40*(3), 103–116.

Purcell-Gates, V., Duke, N. K., & Martineau, J. A. (2007). Learning to read and write genre-specific text: Roles of authentic experience and explicit teaching. *Reading Research Quarterly, 42*(1), 8–45.

Rasinski, T. (2011). The art and science of teaching reading fluency. In D. Lapp & D. Fisher (Eds.), *Handbook of research in teaching the English language arts* (3rd ed., pp. 238–246). New York: Routledge.

Read, C. (1975). *Children's categorization of speech sounds in English.* Urbana, IL: National Council of Teachers of English.

Richards, I. A. (1929). *Practical criticism: A study of literary judgment.* London: Cambridge University Press.

Roskos, K. A., Tabors, P. O., & Leinhart, L. A. (2009). *Oral language and early literacy in preschool: Talking, reading, and writing.* Newark, DE: International Reading Association.

Ross, D., Fisher, D., & Frey, N. (2009). The art of argumentation. *Science and Children, 47*(3), 28–31.

Rossetti, C. (1986). Mix a pancake. In J. Prelutsky (Ed.), *Read-aloud rhymes for the very young* (p. 50). New York: Knopf. (Original work published 1893)

Ruffin, F. E. (2000). *Martin Luther King, Jr. and the march on Washington.* New York: Grosset & Dunlap.

Salahu-Din, D., Persky, H., & Miller, J. (2008). *The nation's report card: Writing 2007.* Washington, DC: U.S. Department of Education, Institute for Educational Sciences.

Samuels, S. J. (2002). Reading fluency: Its development and assessment. In A. E. Farstrup & S. J. Samuels (Eds.), *What research has to say about reading instruction* (3rd ed., pp. 166–183). Newark, DE: International Reading Association.

Santa, C. M, & Havens, L. T. (1995). *Project CRISS: Creating independence through student-owned strategies.* Dubuque, IA: Kendall/Hunt.

Say, A (2000). *The sign painter.* New York: Houghton Mifflin.

Scarborough, H. S. (2001). Connecting early language and literacy to later reading (dis)abilities: Evidence, theory, and practice. In S. B. Neuman & D. K. Dickinson (Eds.), *Handbook for research in early literacy* (pp. 97–110). New York: Guilford Press.

Schmar-Dobler, E. (2003). Reading on the Internet: The link between literacy and technology. *Journal of Adolescent and Adult Literacy, 47*(1), 80–85.

Short, K., Schroeder, J., Kauffman, G., & Kaser, S. (2004). Thoughts from the editors. *Language Arts, 81*(3), 183.

Simmons, J. (2003). Responders are taught, not born. *Journal of Adolescent and Adult Literacy, 48*(8), 684–693.

Soto, G. (1999). Eating while reading. In J. Prelutsky (Ed.), *The 20th century children's poetry treasury* (p. 87). New York: Knopf. (Original work published 1995)

Stanley, D. (1999). *Raising sweetness.* New York: Putnam.

Stauffer, R. G. (1970). *The language experience approach to the teaching of reading.* New York: Harper & Row.

Steig, W. (1971). *Amos and Boris.* New York: Farrar, Straus & Giroux.

Stevens, R. J., & Slavin, R. E. (1995). Effects of a cooperative learning approach in reading and writing on academically handicapped and nonhandicapped students. *Elementary School Journal, 95*, 241–262.

Sticht, T. G., & James, J. H. (1984). Listening and reading. In P. D. Pearson, R. Barr, M. L. Kamil, & P. Mosenthal (Eds.), *Handbook of reading research* (Vol. 1; pp. 293–317). White Plains, NY: Longman.

Stoll, L., Bolam, R., McMahon, A., Wallace, M., & Thomas, S. (2006). Professional learning communities: A review of the literature. *Journal of Educational Change, 7*(4), 221–258.

Tatham, B. (2002). *How animals shed their skin.* New York: Watts.

Templeton, S., Johnston, F. R., Bear, D. R., & Invernizzi, M. R. (2008). *Words their way: Word sorts for derivational relations spellers* (2nd ed.). Upper Saddle River, NJ: Prentice Hall.

Turbill, J., & Bean, W. (2006). *Writing instruction K–6: Understanding process, purpose, audience.* Katonah, NY: Owen.

Vanneman, S. (2011). Note taking as easy as . . . ABC LOU. *School Library Monthly, 27*(4), 23–25.

Vygotsky, L. S. (1978). *Mind in society: The development of higher psychological processes.* Cambridge, MA: Harvard University Press.

Weaver, C. (1996). *Teaching grammar in context.* Portsmouth, NH: Boynton/Cook.

Weber, B. (2004). *Animal disguises.* Boston: Kingfisher.

Wheeler, R. S., & Swords, R. (2006). *Code-switching: Teaching Standard English in urban classrooms.* Urbana, IL: National Council of Teachers of English.

Wick, W. (1997). *A drop of water: A book of science and wonder.* New York: Scholastic.

Wiliam, D. (2007). Content then process: Teacher learning communities in the service of formative assessment. In D. Reeves (Ed.), *Ahead of the curve: The power of assessment to transform teaching and learning* (pp. 183–204). Bloomington, IN: Solution Tree Press.

Wiliam, D. (2011). *Embedded formative assessment.* Bloomington, IN: Solution Tree Press.

Willems, M. (2003). *Don't let the pigeon drive the bus!* New York: Hyperion.

Williams, C., & Lundstrom, R. P. (2007). Strategy instruction during word study and interactive writing activities. *The Reading Teacher, 61*(3), 204–212.

Wood, D. (1998). *How children think and learn* (2nd ed.). Oxford, England: Blackwell.

Yopp, H. K. (1995). A test for assessing phonemic awareness in young children. *The Reading Teacher, 49*(1), 20–29.

Yopp, R. H., & Yopp, H. K. (2004). Preview-predict-confirm: Thinking aloud about the language and content of informational text. *The Reading Teacher, 58*(1), 79–83.

INDEX

Teaching Students to Read Like Detectives
Douglas Fisher, Nancy Frey, and Diane Lapp
Prompt students to become the sophisticated readers, writers, and thinkers they need to be to achieve higher learning. Explore the important relationship between text, learner, and learning, and gain an array of methods to establish critical literacy in a discussion-based and reflective classroom.
BKF499

How to Teach Thinking Skills Within the Common Core
James A. Bellanca, Robin J. Fogarty, and Brian M. Pete
Empower your students to thrive across the curriculum. Packed with examples and tools, this practical guide prepares teachers across all grade levels and content areas to teach the most critical cognitive skills from the Common Core State Standards.
BKF576

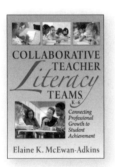

Collaborative Teacher Literacy Teams, K–6
Elaine K. McEwan-Adkins
Explore the work of collaborative literacy teams from their formation to the employment of successful student-focused strategies. Find professional growth units in each chapter that provide educators with the opportunity to discuss key concepts, self-reflect, and remain focused on student achievement.
BKF491

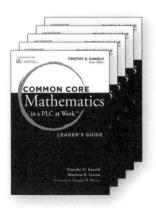

Common Core Mathematics in a PLC at Work™ Series
Edited by Timothy D. Kanold
These teacher guides illustrate how to sustain successful implementation of the Common Core State Standards for Mathematics. Discover what students should learn and how they should learn it at each grade level. Comprehensive and research-affirmed analysis tools and strategies will help you and your collaborative team develop and assess student demonstrations of deep conceptual understanding _and_ procedural fluency.
Joint Publications With the National Council of Teachers of Mathematics
BKF566, BKF568, BKF574, BKF561, BKF559

Solution Tree | Press
a division of
Solution Tree

Visit solution-tree.com or call 800.733.6786 to order.

Wait! Your professional development journey doesn't have to end with the last pages of this book.

We realize improving student learning doesn't happen overnight. And your school or district shouldn't be left to puzzle out all the details of this process alone.

No matter where you are on the journey, we're committed to helping you get to the next stage.

Take advantage of everything from **custom workshops** to **keynote presentations** and **interactive web and video conferencing**. We can even help you develop an action plan tailored to fit your specific needs.

Let's get the conversation started.

Call 888.763.9045 today.

 solution-tree.com

Solution Tree

Solution Tree's mission is to advance the work of our authors. By working with the best researchers and educators worldwide, we strive to be the premier provider of innovative publishing, in-demand events, and inspired professional development designed to transform education to ensure that all students learn.

The mission of the International Reading Association is to promote reading by continuously advancing the quality of literacy instruction and research worldwide.